oic s the

LAKE DISTRICT

VOICES *of the*
LAKE DISTRICT

JANE RENOUF & ROB DAVID

The
History
Press

Cover illustrations, front top: Ambleside Girl Guides celebrating the Guides' Golden Jubilee, 1960. From left to right: Pam Partridge, Helen Roberts, Clover Parsons, two American Guides from Amarillo, Lynne Horrax, Susan Newby. *Below:* Major Porter skating on Rydal Water, 1920s. *Back:* Rose Queen Festival, Ambleside, 1910, in aid of Kendal Hospital.

First published 2011

The History Press
The Mill, Brimscombe Port
Stroud, Gloucestershire, GL5 2QG
www.thehistorypress.co.uk

© Jane Renouf & Rob David, 2011

The right of Jane Renouf & Rob David to be identified as
the Authors of this work has been asserted in accordance with
the Copyrights, Designs and Patents Act 1988.

British Library Cataloguing in Publication Data.
A catalogue record for this book is available from the British Library.

ISBN 978 0 7524 5671 3

Typesetting and origination by The History Press
Printed in Great Britain
Manufacturing managed by Jellyfish Print Solutions Ltd

CONTENTS

ACKNOWLEDGEMENTS

Ambleside Oral History Group would like to thank the respondents or their families for giving permission for the use of the extracts from their interviews in this book. The Group is equally indebted to those who have provided the photographs to illustrate this publication, in particular Joan Newby, whose photographic collection has been heavily drawn upon for this volume. In addition the following people and institutions have provided photographs: Paul Allonby, Another Space and 45 Aid Society (Holocaust Survivors UK), Armitt Museum, Bill Birkett Photo Library, Alec Brood, the Clayton family, Dr Ann Colville, Cumbria County Council, Kendal & Carlisle Libraries and Cumbria Image Bank, Cumberland and Westmorland Archaeological and Antiquarian Society/Mary Fell collection, the David family, John Ellis, the Freiberger family, the Freshwater Biological Association, Carole Hall, the Horrax family, Mary Logan, the Macan family, the Mann family, the MacIver family, Mike Mitchell, Kathryn Nicholson, Sybil Parker, the Porter family, Jane and Paul Renouf, the Rigg family, Judith Shingler, Malcolm Tyson, Maureen Watson, and the Wordsworth Trust.

Ambleside Oral History Group has taken all reasonable steps to obtain permission for the use of all images in this book, but apologises for any omissions which have occurred where owners have been incorrectly identified or could not be traced.

The Group particularly acknowledges the work of historian and author Dr Rob David in compiling the book, and thanks must also go to fellow Group members Barbara Crossley, Pam Kaye, Sybil Parker, Pam Parsons, Allison Peake, Vivienne Rees, Paul and Jane Renouf, Judith Shingler, Fiona Sparrow and all other members who contributed to *Voices of the Lake District*. Our thanks also to Joan Newby and Mary Logan for their helpful advice.

THE AMBLESIDE ORAL HISTORY GROUP

The rapidly-changing world of the 1960s and '70s prompted a small group of people, led by Cynthia Thompson, librarian in charge at Ambleside Library, in conjunction with others, including Jane Renouf and several members of the Rotary Club of Ambleside, to come together and form an oral history group to record accounts of Lake District life before such memories were lost and forgotten. The vision and energy of an early member, Dr Sam Forrester, along with the expertise of oral historian Dr Elizabeth Roberts, ensured that an archive of professional standards was created. Over the past thirty-five years, some 400 recordings have been made by the dozen or so members, which have also been transcribed into written documents for people to read. Although many respondents were living in Ambleside and the adjacent communities at the time of being interviewed, their histories reflect life generally throughout the Lake District as well as their wider experiences, including service in two world wars. The earliest recordings include the voices of those who were able to remember as far back as the 1880s, and the most recent include the newcomers of the twenty-first century, and their accounts cover every aspect of community life and rural society.

During the past few years all recordings have been digitised and in 2006 the Ambleside Oral Archive became the depository of another Lake District oral history project, created by the Lorton and Derwent Fells Local History Society. Their interviews have been added to the Ambleside archive and relate to the life of their communities, with emphasis on the effects of the 2001 Foot and Mouth outbreak. The complete Ambleside archive is available and the texts are fully searchable online at www.aohg.org.uk and at Ambleside Public Library, Kelsick Road, Ambleside, Cumbria, LA22 0BZ (Tel. 015394 32507).

All the voices represented in this book are part of the Ambleside Oral Archive, and are presented as they were recorded, except where the use of square brackets indicates the addition of words or phrases which make the extracts easier to read or provide essential information for the reader.

Our thanks go to all those who so generously shared their memories with us over the years: this book is dedicated to you, and celebrates your lives.

Ambleside Oral History Group, 2011

INTRODUCTION

The Lake District is synonymous with scenery. Its iconic views printed on Kendal Mint Cake wrappers, tablemats or tea towels draw instant recognition at home and abroad. Yet its lakes and crags amount to so much more than mere water and stone, for at the heart of every view are the people who live within it, whose presence has gradually shaped the area from a series of geological accidents and events to a place transformed by human activity. This book is about the lives of people who live in the Lake District, as told in their own words.

The presence of man is visible everywhere, and human enterprise has carved the raw material into today's familiar contours of towns and villages, grazed uplands and wooded valleys, and grand sweeping horizons disected by narrow winding roads and drystone walls. The craggy mountains and the rugged ridges of the central area give way within a relatively short distance to gentler, more rounded slopes. This area of mighty contrasts has attracted countless visitors over the past two centuries, winning it fame the world over, quite disproportionate to its size. The views are unforgettable, with images of awesome magnificence and thrilling natural beauty all contained within an area the size of a pocket handkerchief in the north-west corner of England. Many holidaymakers return as frequent visitors, until the backdrop of mountains, lakes and wonderful walks often becomes the personal background to life's happiest family memories. Since its inception as a National Park in 1951, the beauty of the Lake District is for all to share – and many feel such a strong stake in its continued wellbeing that they willingly give up their time working as unpaid volunteers, helping to restore footpaths, stiles or tumbled walls.

But what of Lake District people themselves? A landscape as outstanding as this has its fair share of extraordinarily talented artists and writers who translate its beauty on paper or canvas. Poets and painters, novelists and naturalists – experts in every art or craft have at one time or another adopted the Lakes as their home. The lives of such local residents as William Wordsworth, Samuel Taylor Coleridge, John Ruskin, Beatrix Potter or Arthur Ransome are well documented. But the everyday stories of those born and brought up among the fells and valleys have gone largely unnoticed and unsung.

Their lives over generations have been far more influential on the fabric of the Lakes, but like ordinary lives everywhere they are rarely chronicled by biographers, or even mentioned in history books. Yet nobody can better recount the dramas and detail of local life, or recall the dying traditions or lost industries. In the path of relentless progress and sweeping social change, technology such as television exposed the most remote areas to world events and mass entertainment. As the isolation of places like the Lake District receded, modern life rapidly eclipsed the past, and with it came greater wealth coupled with new material values and aspirations. It all happened very quickly, and few people thought to capture the ordinary, everyday past. As the very oldest people died, their memories of life in times past died with them, and it was this realisation that prompted interviewers in the Lake District to start their recording work.

The stories told to them illustrate how local people, often by necessity, were both inventive and ingenious, with the practical skills needed to become successful craftsmen or quarrymen, hill farmers or miners, seamstresses, cooks or even aircraft riveters. Accustomed as they were to the curiosity of visitors, local people were friendly and welcoming, with a quick wit and ready wry comment. They had an unspoken and unshakeable confidence that local people knew best in all matters local – and when wartime officialdom demanded such impossibilities as growing crops which locals knew would never ripen, it was quietly outwitted by the farmers, who then carried on exactly as before. In today's communities, where residents are often outnumbered two to one by non-native neighbours, being a 'local' is still important.

Life in the valleys was raw, and was anything but ordinary or boring, punctuated by weather which could be wild and dangerous. The dramatic landscape provided a hard living and employment could be fraught with danger, whether it was quarrying and blasting stone, working with timber, mining for lead or manufacturing gunpowder. Men desperate to earn enough for big families to live on were accidentally killed at work with depressing regularity and many women worked their fingers to the bone in domestic servitude in the big houses. Even children as young as seven were vital to the family economy, earning what pocket money they could delivering milk or running errands.

Yet their hard lives mirror ours in many ways, in the common experiences of childhood, family life and schooldays. Entertainment and sport played a big part in local life, but so too did work and the wages people were paid. The sense of community was strong, bringing people together frequently in annual festivals, fancy dress parades, or as musicians or singers in bands and choirs. Children had somewhere to go almost every night of the week, whether it was Scouts or Guides, boxing or football, bell ringing or country dancing.

One quality shines through the memories of every passing catastrophe or crisis: the stoical, often silent acceptance of the toughness of life, and the ability to carry on regardless, with a complete absence of complaint, or even to turn adversity into opportunity.

Voices of the Lake District celebrates those people whose sturdy robustness imbues the landscape with character and vitality.

one

A SENSE OF PLACE

To outsiders the Lake District is known for its scenery – its lakes and fells – and its weather. It is, of course, a lot more than that. For those who have lived in the area for all or most of their lives, it is also the sense of community and the inhabitants which make it such a special place to live. From this emerges a sense of place which is special and unique, although what makes it so can be difficult to articulate. Times change and memory can play tricks, and it is often the polar opposites – the good old days and the worst of times – that are best remembered. The humdrum has often been forgotten. Bearing in mind this tendency to add colour, what follows are those memories which define the Lake District by the people who live there – the importance of certain events to them, the bonds of family and friendship, the ingenuity and craftsmanship with which they do their work, the natural stoicism which helps turn adversity to advantage, and the love they have of the natural world around them; these Cumbrian characteristics contribute to all that is the Lake District every bit as much as the landscape itself.

It was lovely at Grasmere Sports

We used to go down there [c. 1910] onto the road to watch Lord Lonsdale and all his yellow perils – as we called them – come through. [Lord Lonsdale's fleet of automobiles was painted yellow.] Oh, a whole row of them came through. It was lovely at Grasmere Sports to watch all the lunches laid out, you know, all beautiful lunches, roasted pheasants and that.

Of course we had a shoot at Rydal Hall you know, and Lord Lonsdale used to come to the shoot then. My brother had all the lunches to take up in the cart to a little shooting box of his … past Hart Head and follow the road straight up to Fairfield bottom, and there's a little shooting box on the left-hand side, he used to take all the meals up there, then after he'd taken the meals up he had to go along with the rest of the beaters and beat the pheasants out – and for that you got a brace of pheasants and a couple of rabbits. There were eight in our family and father and mother, I had four brothers and three sisters – but we didn't rely on rabbits and pheasants round about, we had our own sheep and that, and our own poultry.

Margaret Greenup (born 1895)

> *For those returning from the First World War, the peace of the Lake District must have been intoxicating. For some it was not only another world, but also a better one.*

It was a very happy village

In Grasmere we had everything; it was perfect for a village. After the Great War it was a very happy village and although some people thought that we were isolated and rather backward, I can tell you that Grasmere was always very pleasant and busy and we made our own entertainment in those days. We had our local cricket club, which has now gone, a football club which still exists, a good choral society and we took part in the Mary Wakefield music festivals at Kendal. We'd very good tennis courts and bowling green.

We never knew we lived out in the country and were deprived of anything, even in the winter there was always something going on.

Harold Birch (born 1894)

> *Others, however, remember the poverty.*

All the working people had a hard bringing up

In Ambleside there was a terrible lot of poverty, all the working people had a hard bringing up. Bridge Street, there would be families in there, two up two down. They all had big families and some of them had eight or ten kiddies living in there and you know there weren't bunk beds, they were sleeping head to toe, or else on the floor. You'd see them with their washing hanging out – Carr's flour bags, the white ones, from Carr's of Carlisle … well all these people used to get them from the grocer. When the flour bag was empty, you washed them, and they made good pillowcases.

Cecil Otway (born 1910)

Lord Lonsdale handing over the first prize to Ernest Dalzell at Grasmere sports before the First World War. Dalzell won the Guides Race at Grasmere seven times in all, and broke the record on four occasions.

Although Lake District communities did not suffer the extremes of ill-health associated with urban living, rural poverty inevitably led to infant and child mortality. Disease was all too common, and despite the existence of the friendly societies, medicine and medical attention was expensive in an era before the National Health Service. The doctor was a pivotal and often well-loved figure in the remote communities.

Five died with diphtheria in a week

There were fourteen in my father's family, but five died. Five died with diphtheria in a week over the Lake [Windermere] beyond Rusland in the woods. And I've heard Mother say that they came and they burned everything, the beds and everything, and fumigated the house and left them with nothing. And they had to start again from scratch, probably somebody might give them a bit of something.

Mary Kegg (born 1909)

He had often received his fees in kind

Very often the village doctors were singletons in practice, and very set – I don't say 'set in their ways' but they'd been there for a long long time. And they ministered with great diligence and great compassion to the local population. They were much loved. I do remember Ambleside's Dr Johnson with his beard. It is always said that he had often received his fees in kind with bacon and butter and so forth.

Dr Frank Madge (born 1912)

Rich or poor, for many the family was the focus of their lives. Even large families were often close knit, with a real sense of pride in family achievements.

We looked after each other as best we could

In the Great War my father was in the army and he was stationed at Kendal and sometimes at Whitehaven and he was there to train recruits. My eldest brother was called up and he went eventually to India and my second brother was called up and he went to France. He was actually taken prisoner at one time in France. The job of writing to my brothers was given to my brother, Joe, who was the next but one above me. My mother, unfortunately, couldn't write so Joe got the job of doing that. She would just dictate what she had to say and Joe put it down. My sister was in service, private service, at various places in Ambleside. Tom, the next brother to me, started work at the Post Office as Telegraph Boy and graduated to postman and finished up at Windermere. Joseph, he was always in gardening, he started work at The Croft, Clappersgate … then went to work for Mr Grundy at Rydal then to Fox Ghyll until the lady went to Jersey and she asked Joe if he would go with her to look after the garden there, so we lost Joe to Jersey. It was only when he was due to retire that we managed to get him back home. One brother

Above: Dr Johnson and Una Blezzard presenting prizes to the Ambleside Merrylegs dancers.

Right: John Ellis, aged four, with his father in 1914.

died at birth, if I remember right. I never knew much about it at all. I was the youngest and the others helped to look after me. I was luckily born into a very good family. We were very close in every way. We looked after each other as best we could. I never regretted one minute being born into the Ellis family. They were marvellous.

John Ellis (born 1910)

> *Visitors to the Lake District might forget that for local people it is a place of work. Nowadays tourism is the biggest employer, but farming, forestry, quarrying and service industries remain important. In the past the Lake District was the centre for a wide variety of industries. The woodlands supported numerous occupations, and in some valleys mining and quarrying were important. One unusual industry was the manufacture of gunpowder at Elterwater.*

Nor anything that could cause a spark

An 'Albion' was used solely for carrying gunpowder. And it was covered-in specially and took gunpowder from the gunpowder works at Elterwater to Windermere goods yard. The men who worked on that had to wear leather boots; no nails of any sort, and the container in which they kept the gunpowder had to have no sharp edges nor anything that could cause a spark. The gunpowder was packed in boxes and barrels, and from Windermere it went to various quarries round about; even up into Scotland and Yorkshire. Of course the gunpowder was used for blasting. On the return journey, this wagon would bring back charcoal from Windermere goods yard to Elterwater. Charcoal was used in the manufacturing of gunpowder.

Anon. (born 1922)

> *New craft industries were developed.*

Pin money for the local ladies

Ruskin Lace as we know it today didn't actually start with Ruskin Lace, it started as a linen industry, as a cottage industry, and this was established in Elterwater. John Ruskin thought it would be a good idea to revive the spinning and weaving as pin money for the local ladies – it started in 1883 and the ladies called themselves Langdale Linen. The cottages would have an oil lamp which was probably situated over the table and hung from the ceiling. They would have a canopy as a reflector so that all the light from the oil lamp was directed below and that was a much kinder light than our electric ones today.

Elizabeth Prickett (born 1935)

> *Other former industries have almost been forgotten, leaving little or no trace, such as sand dredging from the bed of Lake Windermere. Windermere sand made possible another specialist trade – plastering.*

They used to have these big vacuum boats

Pattinsons, the Windermere firm of builders, was involved in dredging the sand from the floor of the lake. The sand and gravel wharf was set up where the steamboat museum is. They used to have these big vacuum boats, flat-bottomed boats, and they used to have these big pumps on them. They used to suck and pour it into the boats until they nearly sank. Then they'd take them to the Windermere sand and gravel wharf. The small stones were used for garden paths and the sand for concrete and cement.

David Scott (born 1923)

He was very, very good at plastering

Another sand boat belonged to a chap called Bill Bennett between the wars. He was very, very good at plastering and he used to run moulds in plaster of Paris in these big houses, you know, fancy moulds round the ceilings and such like. His sandboat business used to be in Waterhead at the back of Wateredge Hotel. And this sand boat, it used to carry 8 to 10 tons of raw material straight out of the lake. Apparently there was two beds of sand in the west side of Windermere Lake somewhere down below – round about Wray Castle somewhere.

George Braithwaite (born 1910)

> *In the 1960s, Ambleside had a thriving knitting factory known as Cobblestones, long gone but not forgotten.*

The poncho was invented and made in Ambleside

At that time in the late 1950s, early '60s, we had absolutely no trouble recruiting labour, in fact we were never embarrassed by shortages at all. And people were very loyal – they stuck with us because they were getting good money – they were all genuinely local people and they came from Grasmere, Hawkshead and Coniston. The famous, much-lamented poncho in tartan, which was actually the fastest-ever selling trial in Marks and Spencer for many, many years, was invented in Ambleside, not just made but invented and made. But things changed, sadly, as they do, and I would never dream of having a knitting factory here now, because you would never recruit the labour. There's too many other jobs available now to employ a workforce of 120 at that level.

Alex Mann (born 1931)

Laura Richardson (on the left) aged four at 'the other side of the lake'.

Wages were not high and, with limited transport opportunities, for most people their 'world' was defined by their community and the countryside that surrounded it.

Our world was a very small world

It was another world, the other side [of Windermere] because our world was a very small world indeed and until between the two wars, when we got a motorboat, it was a very small world. Sawrey, Hawkshead, Esthwaite and Ambleside – that was our world. Your world was as far as the horse and carriage took you and it didn't take you very far on the other side of the lake really.

Laura Richardson (born 1908)

You'd make the best do you could

Our rent was five bob a week in those days at Lane Foot. Five shillings. The water came from the fell, that was the trouble. We'd no bathroom; it was the front of the fire on a Friday night. And we'd an outside bucket for a toilet. And my husband hated it, he had to empty it. He had to dig a hole in the garden up at the top and empty it. Our landlord was a very mean man … very mean. No one in the village was on mains. One year, I was a fortnight with no water, I used to go and pinch it down at the church, there was a tap down there. I had to go down at night with a big can and carry it up the hill here. You'd make the best do you could.

Anon. (born 1900)

Children knew nothing different, yet living with day-to-day poverty presented its own opportunities to earn a penny or two.

If you saw a rat you'd cut off its tail

There were loads of rats in those days because there were no dustbins ... they were all ash pits and the council wagon used to come round once a week and empty the ash pits. There were earth lavatories which encouraged vermin. If you got a rat tail and took it to the council office you would get 3*d* for it, so if you saw a rat you'd cut off its tail.

Cecil Otway (born 1910)

> *The surrounding landscape was a playground that would have been the envy of urban children.*

I remember seeing a family of otters

When I was a child down there [Coniston lake] it was beautiful meadows, water meadows, and cows and that sort of thing. My recollection of the wildlife down there was marvellous when I was little. There were otters in and around the beck and they nowadays talk about how you never see any otters. Well I remember sitting on the edge of this beck, I used to fish for minnows in a bottle with the ends stove in and I remember seeing a family of otters on the side on the bank at the beck, and I watched them for ages, they didn't see me ... there was a heronry just across the lake, you could see these enormous fir trees with herons on the top, and they used to fish just down beside us and there were flag iris and kingcups.

Barbara Priss (born 1914)

A lot of red squirrels

Round here in Outgate there have always been deer, foxes, badgers and stoats – and a lot of red squirrels, which we used to call Cons.

Len Crossley (born 1915)

> *In spite of the beautiful landscape being part of everyday life, Lake District people have a special appreciation of its magnificence.*

You can't fail to appreciate it

My greatest memories of mountain rescues are of beautiful occasions. Some of the loveliest sunsets I've ever seen have been whilst on a rescue. Or a sunrise when we've been out all night, some of the cloud effects. If there's something very beautiful, however much your mind is on the job, you can't fail to appreciate it.

Sid Cross (born 1913)

> *Living among the hills and lakes brings its fair share of extreme weather, from prolonged snow and ice to sudden flash floods or weeks of unremitting rain or even drought.*

A lady was washed down

The worst that I remember was the 1966 Borrowdale flood when the River Derwent came up to excessive height in just two hours after a thunderstorm. One Saturday evening, about 8 o'clock, the heavens opened and as severe a thunderstorm as you've experienced I think; and the river actually rose up to the village green in Grange and that must have been about 4 feet higher than I've ever seen. Grange bridge was completely under water. The water came up suddenly and just as quickly went down, fortunately, otherwise the bridge might even have been more damaged. The road at Rosthwaite was about 3 feet deep or more and a car in the garage at the Scafell Hotel only had an inch and a half showing above the water. A lady was washed down about a hundred yards from Rosthwaite towards the bridge and someone managed to grab her and pull her out. There was no lives lost as far as humans was concerned, fortunately, but quite a lot of animals.

Alan Mounsey (born 1915)

> *In the past some winters were so cold that snow filled the roads between the walls and the large lakes froze for weeks on end.*

Cumbria floods in November 2009.

I was walking on top of the walls

I was doing the Kirkstone round [in 1940] as a postman and I had to go up there one day when it was snowing, going to the top of Kirkstone Pass is three mile and I couldn't get through, I was walking on top of the walls. And eventually I got through and back again ... and the Home Guard came out looking for me thinking I had been taken prisoner or the Germans had landed!

Joe King (born 1908)

Farming was hit hard in the winter of 1947.

They nearly had to live on fresh air

It was a year when they nearly had to live on fresh air. A lot of sheep died and a lot of lambs died ... over fifty per cent of the lambs would die in the spring of 1947. We used to go round all the fell walls with the dogs and a big long stick to poke in the drifts and see if we could find anything. Some dogs were quite good because they'd tell you when there were sheep under a snowdrift ... some of the sheep were still alive if you got there soon enough. It didn't always work that way. You'd dig them out, they just had to do the best they could then. You'd take food to them at times but 1947 actually followed a very bad summer and there was very little food about. Hay stocks were finished and it was very bad just then.

Connie Thompson (born 1925)

The Old Mill waterwheel, Ambleside, 1940.

The Royal Oak, Ambleside, in the snow in 1940.

We walked across the ice on the lake

I remember once walking across from Waterhead to Ferry House and then back through Hawkshead to Outgate with my mother and we walked across the ice on the lake. There was a lot of skaters then. The last time I walked across Windermere to a pub at Waterhead was in 1963.

Len Crossley (born 1915)

Over the centuries many famous people have made their home in the Lake District. The most famous inhabitant within living memory is probably Beatrix Potter. She is of course well known internationally for her children's stories, and locally for her championship of the Herdwick breed of sheep and her donation of numerous farms to the National Trust. Local people, however, sometimes have other memories.

She was always on our backs, you know

Beatrix Potter couldn't bear to see the local children playing in the village – you know, she seemed to resent it. We played all our ball games in the village street because there was very little traffic then. And when the ball went over into the meadow, and I had to go and retrieve it, nine times out of ten she would be coming along, and she didn't half tell me off. And then she would go to my father and say, 'that youngest daughter of yours is a naughty little girl.' She was always on our backs, you know. We couldn't do this and we couldn't do that. In fact, when we saw her in the car leaving with her chauffeur, we used to raise a cheer and say, 'hooray, she's gone!'

Willow Taylor (born 1923)

There was a fellow called Tut Hudson

There was a fellow called Tut Hudson who used to stand in the middle of Waterhead where the pier is, and he would be standing there with his hand-knitted pullover and embroidered on the front was 'Information Bureau'. He made a living in summer time telling people where to go and stay, and he would fill all the best places, and he got commission.

Brian Crosland (born 1925)

You lost your first teeth on Mammy Dugdale's Claggum

Mammy Dugdale – her house was in Church Street [Ambleside]. It always seemed dark, and you used to go in with your Saturday pennies and she sold this fantastic toffee called Claggum which she used to make in a big iron cauldron. It was like a mint humbug. She used to boil it, and roll it and then she'd put it on a hook and pull it till it got dark brown and light brown. No one could ever make it like she did and we always said it was because she used to spit on her hands to pull the toffee. Then she'd put it into whirls and she had this little toffee hammer and she'd break it up. You lost your first teeth on Mammy Dugdale's Claggum.

Joan Newby (born 1922)

Utilities such as mains electricity and car ownership took time to reach the villages, and in particular the outlying valleys. However, there was no shortage of hands-on engineering skills and ingenuity to access the modern world.

With a tiller to drive it, not a steering wheel

My grandfather owned an electric car [in 1895] which was the only one in the valley, although I believe there was a steam car that somebody else had … he went to work in Fells at Windermere to do hydro-electrics, and this car was an open vehicle, very small with a tiller to drive it, not a steering wheel, and I am almost sure it had solid wheels … He told me he had tried to go down the ferry hill but had to stop because the brakes weren't strong enough to hold the car on the steep part. And he couldn't get up the hill because the engine wasn't powerful enough. He would charge the car's batteries from the dynamo he had put in at Waterside for the electric lights there.

Jean Cutforth (born 1918)

The dynamo house

About the turn of the [twentieth] century he started to build tarns on Claife Heights. He [my grandfather] built dams and got up a head of water and a large pipe went down to the fishery.

He bred brown trout there, and the pipe went on down the field from the hatchery and along the road to Waterside at Esthwaite and then to the dynamo house, which is still there in the garden in front of Waterside by the lake. The engine was kept beautifully polished and bright and lovely to look at. To get the lights on in the house you had to pull a lever to spark the engine and start it running. And when it was fully switched on, and you heard it, the lights came on both in the house and in the dynamo house. And this happened every evening and my grandfather would go out and pull the lever … and before bed it had to be switched off again.

Jean Cutforth (born 1918)

> *Changes came slowly to the Lake District. Early tourism, made possible by the development of the railway system, brought changes, as did the arrival of the first motor buses, and later in the twentieth century the widespread use of cars.*

He drove the 'Yellow Peril'

My father helped my grandfather on the farm and when we came to live in Ambleside he went to the Salutation Hotel and he looked after the horses, I understand. And then from there he started on driving the buses and he drove the 'Yellow Peril', which used to bring the mail from Windermere and all sorts of things like that. They were replaced by the Ribble buses and he drove them. And then there was a Hawkshead bus. One bus went backwards and forwards – sometimes it went to Hawkshead and sometimes it went down to the ferry. He did that for years. The school children from the grammar school used to say, 'Oh Mr Bunting, so-and-so's got a detention, he'll be ten minutes or quarter of an hour,' and my dad used to wait because that was the only bus, you see.

Vera Bunting (born 1920)

Anything that could move, moved

I shall never forget my first Easter here. I started work in the shop on the 1st of March 1959, and Maundy Thursday, my goodness, the traffic down past the shop … and I still say we've never had as much traffic as on that Maundy Thursday. Everybody would get their bangers out you know, there wasn't all this MOT lark there is now and anything that could move, moved. It was terrific – and the amount of money that was spent in those days! We were on top of a boom in 1959 and 1960 and then things started going downhill very quickly.

Alan Hickling (born 1908)

The MacIver electric car at Wanlass Howe in the early 1900s.

'The Yellow Peril' outside the ticket office in Ambleside, 1919.

Ambleside traffic in the 1970s.

> *Language changed partly as a result of the influx of 'offcomers' and visitors, but also as a consequence of changing work practices, access to new media and greater mobility. Not only has the regional dialect become less pronounced, but there has also been a loss of vocabulary associated with activities that have largely ceased. When Braithwaite Rigg talked about his employment in the gunpowder works in Langdale, he used a vocabulary that not many can understand today. This is how he described part of the process of making gunpowder.*

That used to be t'corning house house

There's a wee spot, there is, I think it's a wooden building, aye it is a wooden building.

Well, that used to be t'corning house, then you shunted your stuff back again and up over t'race again and up into t'glazing house. It was glazed overnight, you couldn't bear your hand in't morning, you used to run it, big churns they were, put so much lead in, like powdered graphite, and then that was run overnight, pulled out in't'morning into barrels and taken from there up to t'stalling department. That was stalled all night, dried and then it was shunted off again up top, that was dusting house, to get rid of the dust, t'was like, they were sieved really, they used to rotate like that you know. It shook all t'dust round, it was a dirty job an' that. Same thing applied at t'corning house, t'old fashioned corning house, it used to go round like that but after t'accident they put new machinery in and it used to go backwards and forwards like.

Braithwaite Rigg (born 1903)

> *Until the 1970s tourism was limited to the 'season', and once autumn arrived local people had the area to themselves. In the winter the Lake District reverted to the place that would have been more familiar to earlier generations, although that is not the case now.*

We could all have free ice creams

Ambleside was a peaceful place in winter because everything closed down. No visitors, no hotels open, no fancy goods shops, just the food shops. Waterhead all closed up, no boats out. The last Saturday of the summer season the man with the ice cream left – and we could all have free ice creams.

Joyce Stewart (born 1922)

Father Christmas turns the lights on

Nowadays Ambleside is busy all year round. The shops are open seven days a week and there is no early closing on Thursdays as there used to be. November used to be a quiet time but now it is very busy in the run-up to Christmas, with Ambleside brightened with festive lights and one of the busiest weekends of the year comes in November, when we have a lantern procession and Father Christmas turns the lights on.

Fiona Sparrow (born 1935)

two

THE BIG HOUSE

During the nineteenth century, wealthy industrialists from big cities such as Manchester, Liverpool and Newcastle built large houses in the Lake District, the most popular locations being around the shores of those lakes with nearby rail access to their city homes. Windermere, Coniston and Derwentwater were particularly popular and the architectural design of the big houses reflected the ideas of the Arts and Crafts movement as well as the influence of foreign travel. Some houses were occupied permanently, whilst others were used as holiday homes. All were furnished in the style to which their owners were accustomed and if anything was wanting, they brought it with them. Both adults and children enjoyed a privileged lifestyle, and the local population quickly adapted to their presence and the opportunities it brought for trade and employment.

'We used to love coming': memories of privileged childhoods.

We had a special coach on the train

We came over here [to Balla Wray, near Hawkshead] from Newcastle two or three times a year for two or three months between May and October. We used to love coming, we never cared for Newcastle all that much in the winter. Mother used to get the trunks down from the attics, a round-topped trunk, and some flat trunks a week before we were to come and she used to start packing all these trunks. Into these trunks went the sewing machine, the kitchen paraphernalia, the plated cake stand, the silver teaspoons and all our clothes. On the great day the cart would come up and all the luggage would be piled into the cart and taken down to the station and we went down by tram. It always annoyed me; I thought we should have had a taxi. We had a special coach on the train and into this went the boxes, three servants, the coachman and two horses, so it filled the carriage. Grandmama had a full set of plated silver for Balla Wray, not genuine silver, but I think the bedding and everything else would be still here.

The First World War killed all this elaborate moving from one place to another with the silver egg stands; the first war killed that and a good thing it was too. I can eat my egg out of a china cup.

Laura Richardson (born 1908)

Balla Wray in Edwardian times.

Wanlass Howe.

Wanlass Howe pier with the MacIver family boarding *Dodo*, 1906.

We used to go and pinch all the peaches

We used to go and stay with granny up at The Croft [Clappersgate]; it was a great excitement for us to go. We used to go up by car and we'd probably go for a fortnight every year. When we went there, there were always lots of grown-ups there; uncles and aunts and cousins who looked after us and spoiled us. We came very much into contact with an old lady called Liz – well, she seemed an old lady to us – who I think was probably the head parlour maid and she sort of looked after us as children. She was in charge of us little ones when we went up there, and she had great long skirts on and lovely white aprons and little white hats. My mother never had much to do with us children. I remember that we had breakfast with everybody else, and we would go down to this enormous breakfast, masses of dishes, lovely hot dishes – you turned a cover over, sausages and things all being kept hot, and there seemed to be endless dishes you could choose from. I don't think we were allowed in on any other meal, and as far as I remember we just used to spend the rest of the day having a lovely time. We [my cousin and I] used to play in the lovely woods. We would have lovely games on our own, and then we would go across this bridge that led down to the lower garden, having been told not to spit on the cars below – which we did of course, these lovely open cars which went past, and down below there was this gorgeous garden which led down to the river. Along the wall of the lower garden there were peaches growing, and we used to go and pinch all the peaches. There were boats and although we were very little we were allowed out in these boats, and we'd go down on to Windermere and row up the river and just do what we wanted all day. There was no fear, and nobody was afraid of anything happening.

Joan Dutton (born 1917)

We had a houseboat (Wanlass Howe, Ambleside, 1920s)

Granny [MacIver] had two or three servants in the house – two gardeners and a chauffeur and a nanny, and I think one or two who came in to help in the daytime. It was a big house to look after and she generally had children without their mothers, so they needed a certain amount of looking after. She had a boatlanding with a pier and quite a number of boats where we spent most of the time. We had rowing boats and a centre-board sailing boat, and a houseboat. Granny owned the lakeside and that's where we all used to spend all our time, swimming and boating and playing.

Alison Carrington-Smith (born 1909)

In those days labour was cheap (White Craggs, Clappersgate, early 1900s)

In those days labour was cheap, we could afford maids. We had a cook, parlourmaid, housemaid and a between-maid, and a very precious nanny. After she'd been with us a fortnight she said to mother, 'I'm awfully homesick, I'm afraid I'll have to go,' and mother said, 'Well, stay the month out and see, and if you feel that you must go – we won't persuade you to stop.' Well, at the end of the fortnight she'd settled down and she stayed with us till the day she died forty–eight years later. She was the most precious friend we could have had, one of the family, she was very dear to us all.

Marjorie Acheson (born 1886)

> *'Touch the forelock and stand still': the big house through the eyes of local children.*

They used to bring orchestras and caterers from London

The Storeys of Loughrigg Brow [Ambleside] were [linoleum] manufacturers from Lancashire and they had daughters and a big staff there, with the lodge at the bottom, where their coachman lived. They used to have these balls at the Assembly Rooms, and they used to bring orchestras and caterers from London with waiters. Each year they had a different theme. An Italian at one time, and a Japanese. People were dressed in that style as well, and these dances went on till two or three in the morning.

Alice Brakewell (born 1900)

There were all sorts of do's and don'ts on the estate

I was only quite small, but I remember distinctly going to school from there, walking from Briery Close to Troutbeck Bridge School and there was all sorts of do's and don'ts on the estate. For instance, nobody of the staff, unless it was something very special, was allowed to use the front drive. And if you were a boy and you were about the place and you met any of the family it was always drilled into you that you must make your honours to them, that was touch the forelock and stand still, until they passed by.

George Dobson (born 1907)

> *The beautiful houses and gardens that wealthy families enjoyed were built, designed and maintained by skilled craftsmen, often local to the area. The size of these properties required an army of servants to look after the family and their guests. Being 'in service' meant long hours of toil with only half-day breaks and an annual holiday to look forward to, and living-in gave their employers almost complete control of servants' lives and leisure. The system remained unchallenged until the First World War and its aftermath, when new employment opportunities broadened horizons, especially for women.*

There were thirty-two altogether (Rydal Hall, c. 1905)

They had about thirty-two staff altogether when the Squire was there, all the governesses, the ordinary governess and the French governess and the nanny and the under-nurse, the butler and the footman and three housemaids, the housekeeper, the kitchen maid, the scullery maid,

A liveried coachman outside The County Hotel, Waterhead, 1900s.

and there was a footman, and there were thirty-two altogether, there were three woodmen out in the woods, three gamekeepers, a coachman and a footman and groom, who used to ride on the front with the coachman.

Margaret Greenup (born 1895)

Fancy – sixteen looking after the one lady! (Langdale Chase, 1900s)

There was eight outside and eight inside, sixteen staff altogether. Fancy – sixteen looking after the one lady!

Edith Simpson, formerly Mrs Head (born 1899)

They were a class apart

The owners of Loughrigg Brow, Calgarth – and several other houses between Ambleside and Windermere – employed coachmen and they were a class apart. They were noted for their meticulous appearance. You could pick them out anywhere by their cleanliness and the way they had their hair cut, they were really very, very smart. And they had the horses and everything else turned out well. The hours that they kept were amazing. Father left home six o'clock every morning and didn't arrive home till between nine and ten every night, unless there'd been a dance somewhere. In which case he'd have to take the people to the dance in the coach and wait for them and still go in for six o'clock in the morning.

Alice Brakewell (born 1900)

The men were given a goose and plum pudding for Christmas (Langdale Chase, 1900s)

Every Christmas there used to be a servants' ball, and my father played the fiddle. He hadn't been trained, I don't think he could read music, but he always engaged on the fiddle, always played for a dance; and the men were given a goose and a plum pudding for Christmas, and the ladies were given dress lengths, that was a Christmas gift.

Edith Simpson, formerly Mrs Head (born 1899)

> *Changes in the fortunes of the employing family could cause the servants to be dismissed.*

Mother was a laundress

We moved to Mrs Cunliffe at The Croft [in Clappersgate] when I was three years old in 1903. We had an uncle who had a fish cart and he took our furniture on a fish cart, and I always remember having to sit on it to go up to Clappersgate. We lived at first in the house in the yard. It was a very big yard with the garage and that. Mother was a laundress and my father was Head Gardener. It had a beautiful garden and he had four gardeners under him. When Mrs Cunliffe died abroad our folks had to get out.

Anon. (born 1900)

> *The men who worked for the big country houses and estates as gardeners, woodmen and gamekeepers fared somewhat better than the female staff indoors. The housemaids and kitchen maids slept in the house and were at the beck and call of their employers day and night, under the eagle eye of the mistress. But life outside in the potting shed and the woods was much more relaxed. The head gardener usually lived on the estate in a tied cottage, and led a far more independent existence than staff indoors, largely because his daily movements couldn't be watched at all times out of doors and it was not unusual for the lady of the house to cultivate a knowledge of horticulture and a closer relationship with him than with other servants. The gardens and estate had to provide for the needs of the house as well as support the pretensions of the owners. Coke-fired boilers heated the greenhouses, which provided peaches, grapes and other fine fruits and flowers to grace the dinner party table.*

Every year there was a chrysanthemum tea (Langdale Chase, 1900s)

I was born at the Lodge, Langdale Chase in 1899. My father, who was working for Thomas Mawson, the landscape gardener, got the job as head gardener. He had to pick two more gardeners and they made the Langdale Chase landscape, laid it out and everything in 1890. He looked after the greenhouses by growing peaches and grapes. Mrs Edna Howarth [the owner of Langdale Chase] was very fond of violets, so my father reared them in the garden in frames. Another thing she was very fond of was large chrysanthemums, and every year there was a chrysanthemum tea. Mrs Howarth used to invite the nobility around about to come and view the chrysanths. The servants all had new aprons specially to meet these people, it was a great day.

The outside staff were the three gardeners, the boilerman, the lad, and three coachmen. The little garden boy used to leather the seats – sponge and leather the seats in the garden – you know, if the birds had been round. And another thing which I thought was priceless – there used to be the round grids, you know, on top of the drains – they were blackleaded, can you believe it?

Edith Simpson, formerly Mrs Head (born 1899)

I don't think they were as supervised as we were in the house (Loughrigg Brow, Ambleside, 1920s)

We didn't have anything to do with the staff outside, but we did see the gardener. He used to bring the vegetables in every morning, but apart from that we never saw them much. I don't think they were as supervised as we were in the house, but she kept her eye on everything, she was always roaming round seeing everything was right.

Celia Otway (born 1914)

While you were working you were learning all the time

Miss Harrison was a very, very kind old lady. She was well educated in gardening, and she did actually learn me a lot. I learnt a lot from her, she used to come out and work with you, she knew a lot and she passed it on, and while you were working you were learning all the time, she was telling you the names of different plants and shrubs, their likes and dislikes and so on.

John Todd (born 1914)

The daily delivery to Loughrigg Brow, early 1900s.

> *After the First World War there was often less money available to run big family houses and estates, and servants who returned to their positions had changed expectations and were generally less subservient. However, some families strived to keep the trappings of their country house lifestyles alive, though some found it difficult to come to terms with their straitened circumstances. Family fortunes suffered greatly in the great crash of 1929 and the depression years that followed, and from the 1930s many estates were split up and the big houses sold off to become hotels, private schools and holiday accommodation.*

It was a question of money (Balla Wray, near Hawkshead, 1914-1920s)

We had a governess and one or two servants all through the Great War. But not such high-class servants, they got lower and lower and lower, you might almost call them skivvies, but servants they were. It was a question of money. They wanted higher wages, and Mother, with a growing family and with school coming on, didn't want to pay higher wages …

Our housemaids were all dying for another war because they had been paid so well working making munitions, wasn't this terrible? The war was an eye-opener to them. Before the war they must have got very small pay, although they got housing and very often clothes and good food and all, but that wasn't the same.

Laura Richardson (born 1908)

> *Those houses that survived with reduced numbers of staff often worked them harder than ever to keep up a dying way of life.*

You didn't have set hours; it was all day long, more or less (Loughrigg Brow, Ambleside, 1930s)

You'd all the front steps to scrub, and the stairs, and there were miles of them, carpeted of course, and you'd got to be brushing those with a hand brush and dustpan, no Hoover or anything. Those had to be done by seven o'clock. Then there were other jobs before we had our breakfast at eight in the servants' hall. After that there was the dining room breakfast to see to, and then clearing out, upstairs to the bedrooms and bathrooms which were all to be cleaned. We went on working till one o'clock and then we had lunch and after that was a sort of leisure time if you will, but it wasn't leisure time actually, because you'd got all the darning and mending, sheets and pillowcases to mend and all that sort of thing. You were kept sewing all afternoon, and then there was a time after tea which was post time. You'd got to take the letters to the post – well you got out then, and got a walk.

If the master and mistress were entertaining, dinner was served at eight o'clock, with about eight courses. We had to wait on in the dining room – parlourmaid and I. They'd start off with the first course which would be hors d'oevres, then soup, then a meat course, and then what was called an entree dish in between. This was followed by a fish course and a sweet and a savoury, and then they finished off with fruit, then coffee in the drawing room. It went on till about ten, then you had all your clearing up to do, but it was all part of your duties.

Celia Otway (born 1914)

Vera Isabella Nicholson (on the
right) with another parlour maid
outside Loughrigg Brow, late 1920s.

*Employers still sought to impose old-fashioned paternalism and discipline on their staff, but servants
increasingly flaunted the rules as the old pre-war social order receded.*

We used to meet down in the park (Loughrigg Brow, Ambleside, 1920s)

He was in the Territorials, and came up there [Loughrigg Brow] collecting for something or
other, I don't know what it was, and I answered the door, and that's how I met him. It's a long
time since … you know you weren't supposed to have any followers, and he couldn't come to
the house, so we used to meet down in the park, on my days off, that was the only time. And we
used to meet sometimes when I took the letters to the post, you know, and that was after tea,
but you'd got to be back – I mean you took the letters to the post, you weren't supposed to be
out more than an hour.

Celia Otway (born 1914)

The cook used to let us in (Grasmere private house, 1920s)

Although she wouldn't allow you to go to dances, we did go. We went when they were in bed. We'd go after ten o'clock. The cook used to let us in, you see. We used to make our own dresses. We were all poshed up! They had the dances in Grasmere village hall, and they used to go on till three o'clock in the morning, special big dances, with lovely music.

Elsie Coward (born 1908)

I was the in-between maid (Rydal Mount, 1936)

I went to Rydal Mount when I was fourteen. We had a cook, and a gardener and a handyman. I had left school – I was the in-between maid at that time; I had to help with the washing-up and go down to the croquet pavilion where we made lunches, ham and salad, every day. The house was full of guests. I started work at seven in the morning. Dinner was at half past seven at night and then last thing you did was to take the family a hot drink at ten o'clock. You were expected to be there all the time. When I became a parlour maid I wore a brown silk dress and a coffee-coloured apron and a cap. I earned five shillings a week. I left there in 1939 and got a job as a cook.

Joyce Stewart (born 1922)

> *By the Second World War, most big houses had been divided up into flats or taken over by various institutions, and several of them housed evacuated schools and their pupils during the war years. Since then, many big houses have taken on a new lease of life, restored and refurbished as hotels for the tourist industry and are enjoyed once more for their elegance and beautiful settings.*

The Hall of Langdale Chase after its conversion into a hotel in the 1950s.

three

THE FIRST WORLD WAR

No one could escape the effects of the First World War [1914–1918]. Although the Western Front and other theatres of war were distant from the Lake District, those men and women who joined the forces often found themselves in the front line enduring the horrors of modern warfare, while its impact grew at home. With their breadwinners absent, families struggled to survive poverty and shortage of food, yet the war also gave women significant new opportunities to participate in war work at home and abroad.

> *Predictions that the war would be over within months encouraged many Lake District men to join up, looking for adventure but little knowing what lay ahead.*

It was a pretty tough job

I was sent out to France in January 1915. The first battle we encountered was Ypres, which was a pretty tough job. I was wounded there and sent down the line to Le Havre to a hospital. On coming out of there and being unfit, I was allotted to Admiral Tufnall, who was a landing officer supervising the landing of troops in France. After a spell at Boulogne we moved to Marseilles, where we stayed for some considerable time landing troops from Egypt and a few Russians too. After a while, just before the Battle of the Somme, the authorities knew there was something coming up and they scraped the bottom of the barrel. I had to go for a medical and was passed fit so I had to go and rejoin my regiment in line just in time for the Battle of the Somme. The rest of the war I served with the regiment in the trenches and finished in Germany with the army of occupation. I was demobilised in 1919.

Harold Birch (born 1894)

New recruits photographed in
a Lake District studio.

*Many who worked the Lake District's farms, forests, quarries, mines, bobbin mills and gunpowder works
found themselves in reserved occupations, while others took their particular skills to war. Experienced
blacksmiths were needed at the front to shoe thousands of horses and mules, while amateur musicians could
become military bandsmen.*

You moved the regiment with the band

In those days there was no motor transport to take you to places, you just had to march and
the band was most important, you moved the regiment with the band. You kept them together,
marching, you see because nowadays they have time to go in transport, motor cars, we used
to have to march; march perhaps about thirteen miles a day. France, Étaples, we were training
there for so long, then we went up the line into the trenches. Suchet, Vimy Ridge, and after
Vimy Ridge was the Somme battle. We were in the Somme battle, in Delville wood. I was
wounded at Delville wood – got a little wound in my right arm. I was in hospital for about
a month. Then we came back to the outpost, but I was in the band then, you see. After the
Somme battle word came round that all bandsmen were to be kept out of the line because
there were so many getting wounded and killed so we were kept out of the trenches for a bit.

Billy Nicholson (born 1898)

As casualty numbers rose, recruitment became more urgent.

Go outside and come back again and say you are nineteen

My friend and I were playing football and the policeman came along and said, 'Don't you think it is time you were in the Army?' I was only sixteen! We waited until I was seventeen, went to the recruiting office and we said we wanted to join the Army and go with the Territorials to India. He said, 'Sorry, you'll have to go what they put you in, but we can't take anyone under nineteen.' So the lieutenant said, 'Go outside and come back again and say you are nineteen,' and we were silly enough to do it! Then I wasn't big enough in the chest measurement, half an inch too short. 'Sorry,' he said, 'I can't pass you.' One of the orderlies shoved his finger in the tape. 'I make it 18 inches, that's alright,' so that's how we got away with it. In 1916 we went to India and then to Burma and then as machine gunners in Mesopotamia.

Fred Bowness (born 1898)

Women were now recruited and sent abroad.

Couldn't I go and help them?

After the war had been going on for some time, my father came across a friend of his whose daughter was in France – not a trained nurse but desperately short of help – couldn't I go and help them? And they pleaded and explained how we could help, and so away I went. They didn't want trained nurses but we had to wear uniform and we were under the hospital control … I couldn't even call myself VAD [Voluntary Aid Detachment] 'cos I'd had no training whatsoever and we were there for non-nursing jobs – all the odd jobs that have to be done behind the scenes – and they very soon put me to a convalescent camp in France where the men came to recuperate and to start a mild sort of service training until they got strong enough to do a full day and then they're back up the line.

Katherine Brooke (born 1891)

I was in France before my mother even knew

After the beginning of the war, for a year or two I knitted socks, and then I decided, surely, there's something more than that I can do, and the boy that I was knitting the socks for was killed, and I decided that I would like to join the Army. Well, I went to Preston for interview. They asked you all sorts of questions, silly and otherwise, and that was it. And then I was called up, and that was that. I didn't ask anybody, I was in France before my mother even knew. I felt that as I was single and hadn't any ties I might as well do something. I knew what the war was like; I went out as a clerk and storekeeper but I ended up as a cook and storekeeper. And this was why perhaps we were WAACs [Women's Army Auxiliary Corps] in those days, then Queen Mary decided to have us as Queen Mary's Army Auxiliary Corps so we got a bit of respectability after that! But I think perhaps we didn't have a good name at first because we tipped out men who had cushy jobs at the base, and they had to go up the line, and the girls did the work down below in the offices and cookhouses. This is why the men didn't like us, a lot of them.

Margaret Robinson (born 1893)

> *Despite their role behind the front line, women still found themselves exposed to danger.*

The most awful bomb dropped

Étaples was a training place and a hospital. The Germans warned the government, so they say, [that] if they wouldn't separate hospitals and training, the whole lot would be bombed – and we didn't separate them. The big bombing was in 1917. Three nights running we were bombed; there wasn't a trench ready or anything. Our hut shook so, that was the worst of it, the whole place shook when something dropped, and as I got to the window to tell the soldier outside that tea was ready, the most awful bomb dropped and the whole hut shook – I nearly went over but I grasped something – I mean you were almost off your feet with it. And he fell of course, but when I recovered and things seemed steadier, I went back to the window to tell him and he was lying on the ground, so I thought, 'Oh, he's got hit badly,' but I didn't think he wouldn't get up, but he'd gone. And there was only, well, the wooden structure between us you see. After three nights of bombing at Étaples we had a thousand casualties in that camp and next day I was told five hundred were to be buried and the other five hundred were hospital cases.

Katherine Brooke (born 1891)

> *As casualty numbers rose, the latest list of the fallen would be read out in public for those who couldn't afford a daily newspaper or were unable to read. Even the smallest hamlet began to experience the impact of war.*

Until the men began to get killed, it didn't affect us very much

We were a long way from the war itself and I think really, until the men began to get killed, it didn't affect us very much until food got a bit short. Of course in rural areas, food was never as short as it was in the towns but it affected us, our family, very considerably because my father went straight into the Army immediately [when] war broke out. Having been in the Boer War he had the qualifications and he joined the Westmorland and Cumberland Yeomanry and all young men in the village went in, of course … there are twenty-nine names on the war memorial at Hawkshead from that war, and there are three from the next war. It was the young men that went. We lost them, and a great many were wounded and came back with disabilities of one kind or another and I don't think we had any blinded but we had certain men in wheelchairs for the rest of their lives.

Zaida Macan (born 1908)

We were continually hearing that somebody had gone down

We were rationed for food, and well, all our young friends went to the war. And we were continually hearing that somebody had gone down, and well it was a time of what I call slaughter and heroism, because it was. Fortunately the youngsters didn't know what they were going to … but they were so keen, just as they were in the second war. We were engaged in 1915, and I was inclined to think that we would wait until the war was over and my husband quite agreed, but in 1916 the war was at its worst and it didn't seem as if it was going to be over for so long, [so] we decided to get married. So we did. We had a very quiet wedding; we walked to church and we had no reception. My father sent out notices about the time of the wedding, where it would be, and when it would be, and what time it would be. He said there would be 'no reception but your presence would be appreciated.' So all our friends turned up.

Marjorie Acheson (born 1886)

> *The impact on family life grew, with large families struggling to make ends meet on army pay.*

During the war my mother brought us all up

During the war my mother brought us all up – she had an allowance of eighteen shillings from the government to bring us up – herself and four of us. It was Dad's pay, but he had a separate little allowance when he was in France. He would perhaps use some of it – he didn't get much, but when he came on leave he might bring a few more shillings back with him which he would give to my mother. But you see he had to buy perhaps his cigarettes, and maybe a glass of beer sometimes, and perhaps something else. But she made the 18 shillings stretch. She paid 2/6d rent a week, and then we were all insured – it was one of the things in those days – you insured everyone for death, in case anything happened.

Dorothy Jenkinson (born 1911)

Mother would use all sorts of unspecified parts of pig

Mother found rationing difficult but she had this very old cook who could make things out of nothing at all. She would use all sorts of unspecified parts of pig and turn them into wonderful mince. But we had unlimited milk.

Laura Richardson (born 1908)

It's nothing to be ashamed of because there wasn't any money

During the war everybody had a hard time, everybody's parents were away. I've seen all the lads, they were all working in those days, really, they weren't brought up, they really had a hard bringing up. They lived on lights and sheep's heart and we all did. It's nothing to be ashamed of because there wasn't the money. I've seen all these old ladies having to go out to work to keep their kiddies, you know.

Cecil Otway (born 1910)

Families stretched to the very limit did what they could for the men folk at war. Sphagnum moss was gathered, dried and sent to the front for its healing qualities, while children collected eggs, picked berries and knitted socks.

Jam for the soldiers

I was at school at Winster and during the First World War we used to go round in the dinner hour and collect an egg or two from the farms, and then we used to write our names on them and send them to the soldiers. The farmers used to give them. We used often to get back letters from these soldiers who had had our eggs. We used to put on 'Winster School' you see. We used to pick blackberries; get 3*d* a pound for blackberries, and we used to pick a lot, pick them at nights, you see, and then they used to come and collect them and they were made into jam for the soldiers. We used to knit scarves for the soldiers, these long scarves, khaki scarves, and balaclava things you know, and we knitted a lot.

Mary Kegg (born 1909)

In every Lake District town and village, the signs of war grew ever more visible.

You'd see them knocking about in their blue suits and crutches

I remember at the beginning of the war the refugees who came to Ambleside from Belgium ... also the Artillery used to come through and stay at Knoll Meadow and we used to go at night and watch them tether the horses and put all the gun carriages in ... The wounded soldiers used to come to the Calgarth Ethel Hedley Hospital, which was more for officers, and they used to come [to Ambleside] in their little donkey traps, each wounded soldier had one ... you'd see them knocking about in their blue suits and crutches ... Blacksmiths were working twenty-four hours a day because they were making shoes for the horses going out to France.

Cecil Otway (born 1910)

Some of them were in a terrible state

Calgarth was a private house, and then it was made into a hospital. If I remember right the first lot of soldiers that came there, they were all Belgian and French wounded soldiers. Later on there was lots of soldiers used to come from all over the country and some of them were in a terrible state. As a young lad I used to go across there taking milk, and I got to know some of them, and a lot of them hadn't been wounded by enemy action, but they'd got what they call trench foot.

In the mud of Flanders, day after day, week after week, up to their mid-thigh in wet mud, and their feet began to go like frostbite and some of them had to have their feet amputated.

George Dobson (born 1907)

German prisoners used to come at harvest time.

During the war I can remember distinctly, there was German prisoners who used to come up to Calgarth at harvest time, you know – potatoes – and perhaps twelve of them, there was always a soldier with them, and they used to come up on the train, then walk down [from Windermere Station], then work all day and then walk back and get the train back to Kendal.

George Dobson (born 1907)

As exhausted troops were sent home in the autumn of 1918 and the war drew to its weary close, there was little to celebrate. Many returning soldiers succumbed to Spanish flu.

It was a bad do

I went into hospital in October, about 18th of October. Aye, I had the flu then, it was, oh, a bad do, you know. They were dying all up and down I tell you, that's when I went into Le Tréport Hospital: they thought I was daft like, and lad in t'next bed says 'there's been seven in that bed sin I come in,' he says, 'and they've all died'. That was the one that I was in...

Sam Hoggarth (born 1900)

The deadly flu spread rapidly.

I remember taking jugs of water upstairs

In 1918 Dad was still away in Germany. All our family became ill, my brother and sisters and mother, who was really quite ill. I was eight or nine and ill as well a bit. Everyone stayed in bed, they felt so ill. All they wanted was drinks, and I remember taking jugs of water upstairs for them to drink. I can picture myself up in those bedrooms. We only had two bedrooms. One had an alcove. It was L-shaped was the bedroom, and one bed was down there, another bed that side, and mother's bed here. And I slept with Mother when Dad was not there. My brother had the smaller room. I had to go and get the doctor. No telephones of course, we could not afford them anyway. The doctor came then, and gave them some medicine. Well everyone eventually recovered, although one sister did have bad eyesight through it, but she recovered later. Some people in Ambleside did die of it, yes. But we didn't realise. Of course I didn't realise then what it was, but it was Spanish Flu.

Dorothy Jenkinson (born 1911)

> *Hardship was not the preserve of the poor – even better-off families experienced reduced circumstances.*

When we came back there was very little money

We lived at Field Head. Our condition, which had been fairly affluent I suppose you could say, with three maids and a nanny and all the rest of it and quite a big set-up in the garden – but when we came back there was very little money at all, my father had spent most of his capital on buying horses for the Regiment, for all the Regiment, and of course the war came first as far as he was concerned, we'd got to win it, and everyone had to put everything they had into it including their private means. So when we came back we had our home, of course, but only just one domestic help and one gardener.

Zaida Macan (born 1908)

Headstone mourning the replacement of the Westmorland and Cumberland Yeomanry's 21st Mounted Brigade cavalry horses by bicycles in 1916, when the Brigade was converted to a cycling unit. The headstone is now at the Westmorland and Cumberland Yeomanry Museum at Dalemain House, near Penrith. The inscription reads:

Sacred to the Memory of
Born 30.10.1914: Departed 4.7.1916
Stranger, pause and shed a tear
A Regiment's heart lies buried here
Sickened and died through no disorder
But broken by a staggering order
Our hearts were warm, theirs cold as icicles
To take our horses and give us bicycles
For Cavalry they said, there was no room
So we buried our spurs in this blasted tomb.

The Ordnance gave, the Ordnance
Hath taken away.

Return If Possible

> *Some returning heroes had no jobs to come home to.*

Believe me, the hardship was terrible then

There was a terrible lot of hardship, and the men must have felt resentful about that. They'd given their services and had one hell of a time, and they'd come home to another hell of a time in a way, you might say. They were so hard up, a lot of them, when they came home, men who hadn't jobs to go to … believe me, the hardship was terrible then … really, it was so necessary, was the British Legion then – well, it still is.

Margaret Robinson (born 1893)

> *Armistice Day was created, and the dead honoured with due reverence.*

It was a great sacrifice

As children we were brought up to believe that the Great War was something wonderful and glorious. I now realise it wasn't – for those who sacrificed their lives and for those left to grieve it was anything but glorious.

Joan Newby (born 1922)

Ambleside War Memorial, which records the names of the sixty-nine servicemen and boys who fell during the First World War.

four

CHILDHOOD

In the last century, children of rich and poor families were brought up very differently. Children born into wealthy homes and looked after by a nanny in the nursery experienced separation from their parents, while children in poor families witnessed constant worries about making ends meet. Childhood in those days was far from the idyll often portrayed today, although the freedom with which children played out all day would be unusual nowadays.

Most babies were born at home.

You were usually in bed for three weeks.

You were usually in bed for three weeks. During that time you had strips of white cotton wrapped around your middle and pinned with large safety pins on the front, so that you wouldn't fall apart. The baby was put into a woolly vest. It had little hand-knitted woolly pants. For the nappy there was a huge long flannel thing which was quilted in the body, wrapped over and tied with a thick ribbon, and embroidered round the edge. People used to embroider them for you, with scalloped edges that wrapped over, right over; you turned it up and put a safety pin in it. Then you had a cotton robe and the night ones were like a little nightie, long ones. Over that, a sheet petticoat – a woolly one, a flannel one and then a sheet one, and then the lovely frock made from cotton or lawn. And always a bonnet, so pretty some of them. People took a lot of trouble. Our baby had a bath every day in the evening. Just a round bowl bath on a little table with short legs made by the joiner. You sat on a low upright chair that you cut the legs off to the right height. Then you bathed your baby in this tub.

Phyllis Fothergill (born 1906)

In the early 1900s little boys were often dressed as girls.

Simple toys kept children happy for hours, *c.* 1908.

All she had to concentrate on was the baby

We kept the mothers in bed for several days. It gave the mothers a chance to bond with their babies and the family knew that mum had to stay in bed, so granny and auntie came and made the dinner and mother was treated as something special. She'd had a baby and she was looked after and she had a rest. People brought flowers and everybody ran about after her and somebody came and looked after the kids and it was a real special time. All she had to concentrate on was the baby, to get the breastfeeding established and to rest and to have that initial bonding.

Doreen Smith, Midwife and District Nurse (born 1942)

> *Large families were packed into tiny cottages, with few comforts.*

'Mother t'candle's blown out!'

We lived in a house in Rattle Ghyll. We had an earth closet with the newspaper squares fastened up in a bundle with string at the back of the door. We went out at night with a candle, and if it was a windy night the candle would blow out and then you had to run back in again and shout, 'Mother t'candle's blown out!' and you'd go back into the closet – you'd be sitting there, door shut and wind howling, feared to death of what was going to happen to you and the candle would blow out again ... 'Mother!'

Brian Crosland (born 1925)

I've bathed many a time in a bucket

There were no baths in those days; we all had a bath when our mother had the washing boiler on, when she'd been doing the washing, and you could sit on the edge of the tin bath or else in the dolly tub. I've bathed many a time in a bucket, one leg in a bucket.

Cecil Otway (born 1910)

Children played out all day, and rarely came to harm. Their games relied on improvisation and they found fun in the simplest of things.

We ran free...

We ran free, we played everywhere as children, everywhere. Mother never worried where I was. She said people told her that she need never worry about me getting run over because I always got into the side of the road if I heard a car. Everybody knew me. I had a big teddy bear, and wherever I went, this teddy bear went with me.

Mary Hallatsch (born 1912)

That was how you set off learning to ride a bike

You'd go down the tip and look for two wheels minus tyres. You found a frame and if it had handlebars on, that was great; you didn't bother about a seat because you just wrapped a bit of sack round and then off you went. They went, even though they had no tyres and no saddle. That was how you set off learning to ride a bike. You got on and somebody gave you a push and if you stayed on you were lucky! We used to play in a builder's yard, and it had everything that boys could wish for. There were planks and trestles and during the Great War we made war games with planks and pipes set up on them for big guns and dugouts, it was a boy's paradise.

Percy Middleton (born 1904)

The whole fellside went up

I remember when I was about seven or eight at the end of the summer holidays when the bracken was dead, we made bracken houses, with stakes and bracken threaded through. We liked to cook. One would bring the frying pan, another chips, and another eggs and we would have a fry up. One day the wind got up and blew the fire, setting the bracken alight, and the whole fellside went up. About seventeen sheep were burnt to death and we got an awful scolding but we were too young to be prosecuted.

Len Stephenson (born 1913)

Most children received a Saturday penny or halfpenny pocket money, which bought an entire sticky feast.

You could have so many for a penny

We used to think it was absolutely marvelous what we could buy then, the choice! There used to be little packets of 'kali' [fine sherbet], different sweets, dolly mixtures and coconut macaroons, you could have so many for a penny and so many for a halfpenny. And when you had a penny you could even buy a bar of chocolate and maybe some sweets. Oh we were very, very rich!

Dorothy Parker (born 1922)

Children worked from an early age before or after school, and nobody worried about their safety.

I used to deliver paraffin for Dobson's garage

When I was a lad of seven I was working as an errand boy. I used to deliver paraffin for Dobson's garage. I went to work for a grocer on a Friday night, and he kept his potatoes up in the loft amongst the hay to stop the frost getting at them, and I used to go with a bogey and hurricane lamp up a Jacob's ladder and fill a basket with potatoes and bring it down into the bottom and put it into the bogey. Well, I wasn't big enough to carry this, to bring this basket down, so I used to let it down with a piece of rope in the bottom.

Cecil Otway (born 1910)

When I was six I would milk

When I was six I would milk. We used to separate the milk and churn for butter. What we didn't keep at home went to the grocer in part exchange for some other groceries. When I was twelve I ploughed potatoes up with a plough and a horse.

Margaret Birkett (born 1902)

I could drive a coach-and-four

When I was nine year old I could drive a coach-and-four out of stable yard at Waterhead at Coniston, across road, and pull up at front of Hotel, and turn round for going again – I could do that as good as any man.

George Major (born 1898)

I've made many a penny holding cows' tails

In those days there were no machines for milking – you sat on a milking stool, and of course you got a flick in the eye with a cow's tail. So the farmer would say, 'If you'll hold a cow's tail, I'll give you a penny.' I don't think I got a penny for every single one, but I've made many a penny holding cows' tails, which to us was marvellous, all the things we could buy with a penny!

Mary Hallatsch (born 1912)

They'd give you a ha'penny

One of the things we used to do at Grasmere Sports was to get on a gate. There were three gates coming from Rydal under Loughrigg and you opened and closed gates for people with cars and they'd give you a ha'penny. A ha'penny would get you a bag of Mammy Dugdale's Claggum; it was a noted toffee in Ambleside.

Brian Crosland (born 1925)

> *Older children had more regular work.*

They would stay open until ten

I was eleven when I started work for a shoe-maker, helping in the workshop of a night from school, knocking clog bottoms off, knocking nails out of hob-nailed boots after the shop shut at night, and they used to keep open until eight o'clock every night as long as there was a customer; if there was customers coming in they would stay open until ten.

Cecil Otway (born 1910)

> *Children loved Christmas, but presents were simple and often home-made.*

Anything to fill the stocking up

There was usually in the toe an apple and an orange, and some nuts and some chocolate money. Perhaps a doll for me and a train for me brother. Anything to fill the stocking up.

Abigail Reed (born 1899)

No toys, oh no

With five of us you can imagine. No, we never got any toys or anything like that. I didn't anyway, and I don't think the two elder boys did. You might get an apple and an orange and some nuts and a sugar mouse, you know, something like that. No toys, oh no. Mother couldn't afford toys, no. Half of the time me father was out of work.

Jessie Wilson (born 1911)

Every Easter, children went pace-egging from door-to-door, dressing up as traditional characters.

Old Toss Pot

There was Nelson, there was Old Toss Pot, Mollie Brownbags, there was the Black Moroccan King and The Doctor … and if we were lucky enough to get any eggs, which was the main idea of going, they'd be shared out amongst those who'd performed. We used to perform in front of the houses, knock on the door and see if they were entertained enough to give us any eggs or cash.

John Ellis (born 1910)

The eggs were taken home and hard-boiled.

They used to come out all coloured and stained

We used to get onion peelings particularly, only the skins and perhaps some green plants or flowers out of the garden, wrap them all round the eggs and wrap round with cloth, tie them up and put them into a big pan and boil them up. They used to come out all coloured and stained, then we would take them out and roll them. We went up as far as the top of Wansfell and roll them from there until we got a winner.

May Bowness (born 1901)

The Lake District year was punctuated by community events such as Rushbearing, galas, fancy-dress parades and sports day. Scouts, Guides, choirs and bands and organisations such as the Girls' Friendly Society met weekly.

She used to sit there with mittens on

The maid brought the tea in beautiful cups and saucers on a tray. Miss Bolland was sweet. She used to sit there with mittens on. I've got a pair of her mittens, lace mittens, and a little cap and she would read us a story while she sewed. It was all the Girls' Friendly Society.

Mary Hallatsch (born 1912)

Performance of Pace Egging play at Grasmere between the wars. (Courtesy of The Wordsworth Trust)

The belfry at St Mary's Church, Ambleside. The bells are the fourth heaviest ring of bells in the United Kingdom, with the heaviest (tenor) bell weighing 32½cwts.

I was very nervous at just fifteen

We had to start ringing at half-past five in the morning on Christmas Day. I got up in the tower house feeling very proud of having gone down in the dark. There were no lights so I had to have a torch, and it could be very frosty and slippery. I thought, 'I hope there's someone there.' I was very nervous at just fifteen. So I took a run up the tower, sixty-one steps right to the top, and I had to stand by a ringer and if there were eight ringers, I didn't get to ring. This particular Christmas morning at half-past five there were only seven, so I went in. I've never been so nervous in my life. I was in Town Band twice a week, bell ringing twice a week. We used to learn all-in wrestling and go down to the YMCA and play billiards and snooker, of a night.

Alan Capstick (born 1910)

They don't have socials these days

The thing I remember – there were lots of social evenings. But of course they don't have socials these days. But a social was something you went to before you went to big dances. It would consist of dancing and people doing turns or singing or little sketches sometimes and then supper. I think I was about twelve or thirteen probably when I was taken to my first one, which was big, it was grown up.

Joan Newby (born 1922)

> *Children raised in orphanages experienced a very different childhood.*

We wore clogs and a cloak

We were singled out. My first recollection of our clothing – we were all in this crocodile, marching through Ambleside, we wore clogs and a cloak and we weren't allowed to just stroll through … We had one matron that was really very cruel and the teachers were very helpful, and they got rid of her because she was so cruel. She used to mark some of the girls, you know, with the punishments, and the teachers noticed … smack us with the back of a hair brush, and the wooden spoon which left bruises on our legs … we grew up being told we were different, we spent our life saying thank you, we had to be grateful.

Kathleen Anderson (born 1936)

We enjoyed life because we were children

We enjoyed life because we were children, we had the energy of children, we didn't know anything different as children, we thought the food was what everybody else had, we liked the part because that's all we knew. It's only later on, when I got to sixteen, seventeen, then the doubts, the worries, the wondering and the questions started. It was quite a hard time, trying to work out where you sort of belonged.

Kathleen Anderson (born 1936)

You worked either in the house or the kitchen or you waited on the staff

There were about eighty girls and we had our own classrooms and dining rooms and a huge kitchen. I saw my mother when I was thirteen. She had married again and had three more children. Once a year I was allowed to see my brother … I left school when I was fourteen in 1944 and became a house girl. You worked either in the house or in the kitchen or you waited on the staff. We still had to wear uniform – long brown capes with hoods and brown gym slips. Even our summer dresses were brown and cream and we had blazers. We'd got out of wearing lace-up boots and wore ordinary shoes. House girls got three half days holiday a week and a shilling a month spending money. We bought toilet soap because we used carbolic soap and tooth powder in the orphanage so Palmolive soap and toothpaste were gorgeous.

Then the older ones were found jobs, and we just were looked after by the Home, clothed and fed, until we were old enough to go out to work. That was the main intentions of the Home, to have us all highly trained and well able to do cooking, cleaning, housework in general, so you could be a domestic servant.

My mother died when I was fifteen. It does affect you. You go through life craving for people to like you and being brought up in an orphanage you haven't really got self-confidence because you've always been told to do everything … you get punished if you disobey, a belt across the head. We were punished severely, shut in cupboards … and the same food shoved in front of you for three days if you didn't eat it.

Nancy Maher (born 1930)

> *Although Lake District children enjoyed the benefits of fresh food and clean air, there were occasional outbreaks of diphtheria, tuberculosis, scarlet fever and polio, alongside the more common childhood illnesses such as mumps and measles. Before the National Health Service was introduced, families paid for the doctor by insuring themselves through friendly societies such as the Oddfellows, or subscribed to a doctor's club.*

He concocted his own medicine

We were in a doctor's club. We used to pay ten shillings a month, and then you got a free doctor, that was all you got, and he concocted his own medicine. There were no prescriptions or clinics or anything like that in those days!

Tom Coates (born 1902)

Children with infectious diseases were isolated for weeks.

You talked to them through the window

I remember people with scarlet fever going to the building at the top of Dunmail Raise, I remember my girlfriend at school, Jane Sarginson, had scarlet fever, and I remember going to visit … you talked to them through the window from outside. I think there were only two or three out of one family had scarlet fever, and two had diphtheria. But we were alright. We had measles and mumps and chickenpox, but we never had anything else, but you know, living on the farm we had good food and plenty of milk and everything.

Tom Coates (born 1902)

We didn't catch things

Because we all lived in an isolated valley [at Wythburn, Thirlmere], apart from a bad cold here and there, we didn't catch these things that you always catch from one another. I had whooping cough when I was ten and I got that from the children next door because they'd brought it from Grasmere where their grandmother lived.

Martha Hart (born 1913)

Dentistry could be painful.

Was I glad to get out of there!

Dr Allen was at Hawkshead. He used to pull your teeth out as well. I can remember going along once, my tooth was a bit slack, and he said sit down there and he pulled it out there and then. He didn't put anything in it. Was I glad to get out of there! It cost you one shilling, I remember that.

Len Crossley (born 1915)

I had every tooth taken out

All my teeth went very bad and one day this car came up home and then another car and me Mother says, 'Go into the house,' and I had to lay on the table with a cushion under my head and the doctor just emptied the bottle and he poured it on, it was chloroform, which I didn't know, and he poured it out onto a lump of cottonwool and he says, 'Can you count?' and just put it onto me nose, and when I woke up I wondered what my mouth was bleeding for, but I had every tooth taken out.

Tom Nicholson (born 1927)

> *Children were dosed with traditional remedies.*

We spent nearly all Saturday round in the loos

And then out came the medicine, which consisted of cod liver oil, malt, a little black pill, and Parrish's chemical food, all in one dose. And this was Friday night, and we spent nearly all Saturday round in the loos … we did have a lot of cod liver oil, but it was raw, it was on a spoon. Cascara, caster oil sometimes, if we were caught scrumping!

Kathleen Anderson (born 1936)

> *Lake District childhood gradually changed as families had fewer children and increased income. In common with national trends, children roamed less freely as traffic increased, television provided their indoor entertainment and greater mobility widened their horizons far beyond those of their parents.*

five

EDUCATION

In an area such as the Lake District there were village schools in every valley. Boys and girls started infant school at about four years old and progressed to elementary education at about eight, normally leaving at fourteen. Relatively few pupils gained scholarships to grammar school, which existed in a few of the larger towns, and often families could not meet the extra expense. The sons and daughters of the richer families who had built their homes in the Lake District were usually educated at home by governesses before being sent to boarding school. There were also quite a number of small private prep schools locally, coaching for entry to public school, and a teachers' training college in Ambleside, which also had a small practice school attached. Then, in the 1960s, children's educational opportunities changed completely with the advent of the comprehensive system.

The majority of people were poor

I can remember in the [Ambleside] Infants' School riding on a wooden horse, a rocking horse … and playing in the sand … and the little lavatories with tiny seats … and the parties we used to have at Christmas time. We were all asked what present we wanted for Christmas left under the great big Christmas tree and I always used to ask for a joiner's set. The majority of the people who went to that school [Ambleside] were poor. The wealthy people never went to that school, they all went to private schools.

Brian Crosland (born 1925)

There was no nonsense at all

It was pretty tough, I'll tell you; there was no nonsense at all. They were very pleasant but very, very stern: they would stand no nonsense, even at that age. You knew where your place was when you were in the Infants' School and Miss Routledge, the head teacher, was a very kindly person, a wonderful person, but she was stern over many things.

The rocking horse from
Ambleside Infants' School
(now at the Armitt Museum
and Library, Ambleside).

A group of pupils at Ambleside Infants' School, 1922. Miss Routledge, the headteacher, is on the right.

They had a little table and when you saw that table you remembered how, in turn, one time or another, you all got leaned over there and given a few whacks when you were in the Infants' School: there was no messing. It was enough just to remind you that you had to fall in line.

William Thornborough, pupil (born 1919)

That squeak will live with me always

If you sat at all, you had your arms folded and you weren't allowed to move, and if you fidgeted you had to sit with your hands on your heads, or with your arms behind your back folded. And we sat like that for half an hour, it really was terrible. And we weren't on comfortable chairs that fit your contours, we were on a long desk seating eight on an iron framework and the desk in front was hinged onto a seat so there was no give anywhere. And the seat used to become very, very hard by the end of half an hour and you were dying to put your elbows on the desk and of course you daren't let your hands stray anywhere near. Oh, the great joy of being inkwell monitor. You got an hour off on Friday afternoons. And you'd to take all the inkwells, put them in the inkwell tray, pour all the ink out that was left in, and wash each individual inkwell and turn it upside down to dry. And on Monday morning you refilled them and delivered them out again. We all had broad nibbed pens. We started on slates – oh that squeak will live with me always.

Teacher used to make treacle toffee on the stove on cold winter afternoons, we all got a piece. They don't do that now, do they!

Three of the teachers lived in the schoolhouse and we went in, in groups, and did the housework for them, taught from scratch you see, the proper way to clean windows, the proper way to clean brasses, the proper way to set the table and everything like that. We were also taught table linen and darning – it was terribly difficult. The vicar had seven sons, and we used to darn all their socks at school, stockings and socks for a family of seven and they had to be done beautifully and we used to resent this a bit – the vicar in those days had a staff, you see, my mother used to say she could do with a bit of help with her darning! Why couldn't we take our socks to school to darn, it would still be practical. But we'd to do the vicar's sons.

Alice Brakewell, pupil and latterly a Supply Headteacher (born 1900)

We had a Christmas pudding

At Christmas time we had Christmas pudding. We all took something, flour, sugar, eggs fruit … [Miss Routledge] always had this huge tree and there was a present for every child under the tree … we'd have a bowl of Christmas pudding with custard on it, they used to say she cooked it in the boiler room … and we'd all sit there waiting for Father Christmas to come. I never knew how she got the money, how did Miss Routledge raise the money for all those presents that we all got?

Joyce Stewart (born 1922)

> *Keeping the schools open during the cold, dark winters was a constant challenge.*

Nobody suffered, nobody grumbled

Langdale School was warmed by two huge cast-iron fires. If you happened to be near them you were warm; if you happened to be at the other end of the room you suffered the cold in silence, and said nothing about it because it wouldn't have made any difference.

They were open stoves really, quite large to give a good surface heating area, and of course lighting was by oil lamps because we did not get electricity in the valley until 1955. Nobody suffered, nobody grumbled, and I personally look back on my school days with joy, the greatest joy. I never had a dull moment.

John Holmes, pupil (born 1916)

> *Children helped keep the classrooms neat and clean.*

Every Friday afternoon we got out our polish

Miss Routledge had the Standard Fives in what was then the only big room. The classroom looked very trim and very tidy. Every Friday afternoon we got out our polish and polished each individual desk and made it even more trim and tidy. But we did our bit, it was part of our education.

Mary Thompson, pupil and latterly Headteacher (born 1911)

We always kept our schools looking like a drawing room

We always kept our schools looking like a drawing room nearly, but nowadays they always seem very untidy to me … and of course the children walking about and talking to each other, they never thought or dared to do such a thing in our time.

Alice Blezzard, Headteacher (born 1880)

> *At the beginning of the twentieth century the school curriculum looked very different.*

I trained my children to say 'Madam'

It was extremely strict at Ambleside village school. Scholars were seated in long parallel desks which held four or six, with backs upright, no fluttering hands or scraping feet, speaking only by permission and addressing the teacher as Sir or Ma'am. I didn't like this Ma'am, I trained my children to say 'Madam' and they took to it quite naturally.

Miss Blezzard

It was a real sing-song

… we were all saying twice one are two, twice two are four … and it was a real sing-song. They started long multiplication and division in Standard Three, that was when they were nine years old, then in Standard Four length, weight and time and the compound rules. And then in the upper classes they got to simple and compound interest, money problems, stocks and shares. If a child couldn't read fairly fluently by the age of eight they were considered below par and given special attention. Reading aloud in turn was the regular practice, the children could therefore judge each other and some would work very hard to keep as good a show as their classmates.

Miss Blezzard (born 1880)

Children walked considerable distances to school, and some even walked home at dinnertime.

They were hardly ever late

Some children who came to Ambleside village school walked enormous distances on foot. In winter we closed at three o'clock to let those children get home. They walked every day and were hardly ever absent or late.

Miss Blezzard (born 1880)

Classroom at Ambleside Infants' School, Christmas 1927.

I carried her on my back

I can remember one child coming to school through the snow, and the snow fell all day and at four o'clock it was getting dark, and it was nearly impossible I thought, this child will be buried under it. I carried her on my back, I think about three quarters of a mile. I was in a state when I got back home again, nearly put my back out, that child.

Alice Brakewell, Supply Headteacher (born 1900)

> *Teachers tried to make education relevant to their pupils.*

The children were learning something sensible

I was asked, 'Why do you want to teach woodwork?' I said, 'Well, all these boys are going on to farms when they leave school, and there's nothing else for them, no mills, factories, anything, and they'll need to make their own gates or chicken coops and do repairs on the woodwork already there, it's just so that they can use their tools.' It seemed to me to be practical and so it turned out. The fathers were pleased because the children were learning something sensible.

Miss Brakewell

We used to translate into sheep

This one particular boy – ten take away two – no, couldn't do it … and then I discovered, well, he can do sheep. So I said, 'Well, you know, father's got ten sheep in the field, and two got out. How many are left?' 'Eight.' 'Yes,' I said, 'you can do it, you see.' So after that we used to translate into sheep.

Miss Brakewell

> *You could become a teacher, either through becoming a pupil teacher or alternatively going to grammar school followed by a teacher training college.*

Religious knowledge came high on the agenda

You could go to the grammar school and then take a year's student teachership and then go to college. But I hadn't been to the grammar school, so I could stay on at the school I was attending from fourteen to eighteen as a pupil teacher, learning how to teach, but not getting the different subjects, no maths or French or German. So mother said she would rather I went to the grammar school and did the thing properly and then go to college. And so I went to the grammar school and I had to cram into that [one] year what the others had done from eleven to sixteen. You had to qualify in English, Maths, Geography, History, French and Latin, and

Alice Brakewell.

Fairfield Practice School in the 1920s.

Religious Knowledge came high on the agenda, you'd to be good at that. We'd to take a special Archbishop's exam for that because most of the [Westmorland] schools were Church schools.

Miss Brakewell

Cheap labour

I became what we call a pupil teacher. In those days it was customary all over the country to have cheap labour. And that was how they got their teachers really. You became a pupil teacher at fourteen. And then that meant that you were supposed to teach half time and study half time. But it meant really you had a group of children – you went on all day really, I didn't have much free time. And then you had a certain amount of tuition from the teacher. Well, I did a lot of my work through correspondence courses about various subjects.

Gwen Hall, Headteacher (born 1905)

Ambleside was the home of the Charlotte Mason College of Education (teacher training) but it did not prepare students for teaching in state schools. The young women at the college had been privately educated and were trained to teach in schools similar to Fairfield, the College's own practice school.

Four or five children in each class

Fairfield was the practising school, and when we did our teaching, we would have to go down to Fairfield all day and take a form. The headmistress in our time [1928] would come round and see how the lessons were going, you used to teach four or five children in each class.

Miss Molyneaux, student teacher (born c. 1910)

I don't know how the students were selected

Charlotte Mason was elitist in the sense of the selection of the students, and in what they were aiming for their students to do. I don't know how the students were selected, but we all came from pretty good, affluent middle-class backgrounds ... and highly selective schools. And we certainly were trained only to teach in that sector of the system. I wanted to teach in an ordinary straightforward primary school, but I was not considered qualified.

What we learnt reflected Miss Mason's educational philosophy ... to help children to think for themselves, to learn to concentrate, to be selective in what they learned. We also had nature walks and bird walks, they were compulsory. And twice a week we had to do a thing called a nature notebook. Throughout the two years you were expected to paint, draw, observe, write about flowers, birds, any kind of natural phenomena and they had to be listed with their Latin names. We had to learn Greek, and read the New Testament in Greek. What did stick was Plato. We ploughed our way through *The Republic* ... but in hindsight you wonder why twenty girls – I was only seventeen at the time – should sit down and solemnly plough their way through Plato!

Josephine Dunn, student teacher (born 1924)

Pupils at Fairfield Practice School experienced an ever-changing variety of student teachers and a rather limited education.

It was very old fashioned

The school, which was separate, was staffed by a few permanent staff, but teachers were students from the college. It was the training college for the whole system of PNEU [Parents' National Education Union] schools which operated throughout England, but also it was designed for diplomatic or service families who were abroad and could follow the curriculum in England, with the books and tuition at home. So that when they came back to school in England they were at the same level as all their contemporaries. It was very old fashioned. I think the books were Victorian ... there were no sciences apart from Nature Study.

Jennifer Forsythe, pupil (born 1931)

> *Many of the village schools in the Lake District expanded enormously at the start of the Second World War when the area hosted evacuees from the North East and later from London.*

They turned out into rosy little children

Up to 1939 we had about sixty children at Troutbeck and then during the Second World War, 123. I remember putting up this number on the number board. Those were evacuees from Jarrow and Newcastle and poor little things, they came lost. They were there four or five years of course and they turned out into rosy little children and they became little country children.

Alice Blezzard, headteacher (born 1880)

They'd come as a school

When the war came, that made a lot of difference because there were so many evacuees and we were only in the place half a day, and then we had to clear out and go into the Conservative Club and then let the evacuees have the school for half a day and it was very hard going.

Peggy Walker, teacher (born 1922)

> *Private schools flooded into the area.*

Grasmere was full to bursting

I had a part-time job in a private school – private schools evacuated themselves – you couldn't get accommodation really anywhere because all the big houses had been taken over by private schools – and Grasmere was full to bursting.

Meg Walker, teacher (born 1921)

> *There were also small privately-run prep schools to coach children from better-off families for the Common Entrance examination for public schools or for scholarships to grammar schools.*

Maybe six or eight to a class

There were two Miss Herds – and they both taught different subjects and were very strict … They were noted in the community for having a very high success rate with people going through the exam and they were very small classes, maybe six or eight to a class, and it was very interesting because they had travelled extensively around the world and they had all kinds of artefacts in their home from these travels, so geography or history became very realistic.

Fred Freiberger, pupil (born 1938)

Marjorie Frost, a Kelsick Grammar
School pupil in her uniform.

You tended to get rather strange teaching

All private schools in the [Second World] war were a bit zany because, you know, the teachers
were people who for one reason or another (one never knew exactly why) weren't involved in
the war and so you tended to get rather strange teaching. But of course there were also things
like corporal punishment. I remember being caned with a cricket stump for teasing someone –
in an unfair manner, and that wasn't unusual. There must have been something like a hundred;
the King's School, Ambleside was quite a small school even by the standards of that time.
I learnt to play cricket, there was a lot of activity going on and I remember learning strange
things like being taught the Pythagoras theorem at the age of about eight, but I didn't encounter
it again until the age of about fourteen.

David Buck, private school pupil (born 1934)

> *Older pupils at elementary school had to earn the right to a secondary education.*

You'd to pass the scholarship

When they built the new Kelsick Grammar School [Ambleside] up the hill in 1907 it was a fee-paying school but there would be some free places, but you'd got to pass an 11-plus to get in. It was called in those days 'the scholarship'. You'd to pass 'the scholarship'. It was for boys originally, but later they admitted girls.

Walter Annis, teacher (born 1907)

I was determined to go to the Kelsick Grammar School

I was determined to go to the Kelsick Grammar School and I got the County Scholarship. I had my dinners paid for me because not many could afford to buy them at one shilling a day! The uniform was a navy blue gymslip, white blouse, black stockings and shoes, yellow girdle and a black and yellow tie, and a blazer and a funny pudding basin hat. Summer – a blue dress with white collar, and a panama hat.

Joan Newby, pupil (born 1922)

Being the eldest of nine children, my parents couldn't afford it

I sat my 11-plus and passed it, but I couldn't go to grammar school because I had to go to Ulverston because I lived in Lancashire – and that meant boarding out in Ulverston – and being the eldest of nine children my parents couldn't afford it. So I stayed on at Skelwith School until I was thirteen and a half when I was allowed to leave school because they couldn't teach me any further and I got employment with George Gatey & Sons, Solicitors, in Church Street [Ambleside] and I was with them until I was seventeen. I could see that there was no promotion at all, it was a dead-end job. I was waiting for dead-men's shoes and I left and went into the grocery trade, like my father.

Len Stephenson, pupil (born 1913)

> *The arrival of comprehensive education in the 1960s opened up new horizons, especially for country children whose only previous chance of eventual access to higher education or a professional qualification came and went briefly at the age of eleven through a scholarship to grammar school for the lucky few.*
> *Then, in 1965, local grammar school selection and secondary education changed dramatically with the opening of one of the the country's earliest purpose-built comprehensive schools, at Troutbeck Bridge. Children welcomed their new and extremely well-equipped school, but for many it was also the end of an era with the closure of The Kelsick Grammar School, Windermere Boys' and Girls' Grammar Schools and the elementary schools.*

This new mixed school

Certainly when the Lakes School started it was regarded as a beacon for some of the other schools; there was an enormous number of people who came to see it … it was one of the first purpose-built comprehensive schools – that was the tremendous advantage and it is all on such a wonderful site.

We got the comprehensive school agreed to by the Education Committee, and then it was a case of getting these three schools to merge, but each school had its own history, its own values and fortunately they were very good schools, and I think possibly one of the biggest tasks was to get children to remember their old schools with affection and pride, but transfer it to this new mixed school. And then of course we grew, and not only grew but the buildings grew too.

Griffith Thomas, Lakes School first Headteacher (born 1917)

Prior to the introduction of the comprehensive system, pupils who had failed the 11-plus examination had to stay on at school until they were fifteen, but there was little curriculum for them. This teacher at first resisted a move to the Lakes School.

Something had to be done for those boys

I decided in my own mind that it was the right move. I'd been against it but I was wrong. The county had got to do something about two things. One was that they had raised the school age to fifteen, and the lads in the Ambleside village school got nothing, and they got woodwork by coming up to Kelsick one afternoon a week, that was all they got in practical work. Something had to be done for those boys. Sport and music improved and of course it became very strong at the Lakes, and there was much more land to play games on, and there was a proper gym, and excellent woodwork and metal work and so on, and first rate cookery equipment. The people who gained most from going to the Lakes School were those who failed to get in the Grammar School – the lads left behind at Ambleside and the girls in the Old College [Windermere].

Walter Annis, teacher at Kelsick Grammar School and the Lakes School (born 1907)

The new opportunity of staying into the sixth form allowed scores of children, who would previously have left elementary school without qualifications at fourteen, to go to college or university. However, many graduates then found it impossible to get local jobs commensurate with their degrees, and have left families and friends behind to settle elsewhere.

six

AT WORK

In the twentieth century. jobs in the Lake District were fairly plentiful but rarely well paid, offering a variety of employment opportunities, though more so for men than women. Most villages were until recently largely self-sufficient so there was work to be had in the shops, as tradesmen, and in the professions. Earlier in the century wealthy residents of the big houses provided many jobs in service, and tourism gave opportunities to work in hotels and lodging houses, laundries, cafés and bakeries, or running pleasure trips. Jobs in the traditional occupations of farming, quarrying, mining and forestry fluctuated according to the economy. More recently tourist related occupations have increased both in number and in variety, employment opportunities have continued in farming, forestry and quarrying, and a small number of highly skilled jobs in the arts and sciences have also become established.

> *Those children who did not go to grammar school started work full time at fourteen.*

Every bit hand-made

We were making hand-made shoes and I started when I was fourteen making shoes and clogs and farmers boots and we made them for £2 10s. Every bit hand-made. Then I went to Horrax's bobbin mill at Stock Ghyll for 17/- a week making bobbins, peeling poles. Then I worked for my father chipping and tarring roads and we had a coal business delivering coal. Then I started for myself making shoes.

Cecil Otway (born 1910)

Everything had to be weighed

We used to have a travelling shop when I started work [at Ambleside Co-op]. I used to go out with the driver. The travelling shop was fitted with trays stacking as many goods as we could of all descriptions. On Mondays to Wednesdays we went to all the surrounding villages.

Harry Turner outside
Turner's grocer and
confectioners shop,
Chapel Hill, Ambleside.

Cecil Otway still making
boots in his workshop
in Ambleside in his
nineties. (Photograph by
kind permission of Paul
Allonby)

On Thursdays we were in with the rest of the staff bagging and weighing everything into pounds and half pounds. Everything had to be weighed. There was no pre-packaging. Thursday was our half day and we worked until one o'clock. On other days we started work at 8 o'clock and finished at 6. On Saturdays we worked till 7. We used to get one week's holiday a year.

John Ellis (born 1910)

> *With ready supplies of renewable energy from local timber and water, mills provided employment for men, and latterly women. In 1902 Horrax's Bobbin Mill opened a laundry, serving the big houses and hotels.*

We did the laundry for the Queen of Holland

There used to a be a waterwheel, but that wasn't sufficient power and so they installed a large steam engine and we ran the two together. The laundry went right as far as Grange and Windermere. We used to do the laundry for all the big houses, then the big houses closed, and we had to go further afield to find customers. We used to do most of the hotel work in the district. Everything had to be done properly because we were supposed to be tip-top. We did the laundry for the Queen of Holland when she came to stay here at Rydal Hall in about 1931. I should think we employed between twenty and thirty girls. We worked from six to six, and thought it was marvellous when Saturday was a half-day. By jove we were on the high road then, a half-day on Saturday!

Bernard Horrax, mill and laundry owner (born 1896)

It took about three quarters of an hour to get a stiff shirt highly polished

It was a high class laundry. We used to do stiff shirt-fronts and collars, it was mostly for the gentry. The shirts were washed and then you'd starch the fronts and it took about three quarters of an hour to get a stiff shirt highly polished.

Anne Dugdale (born 1934)

> *Enterprising women took in washing on their own account.*

They used a lot of starch

Monday and Tuesday were wash days. They used to finish washing round about the middle of the afternoon, then me mother used to do her own washing in what was left of the water. The rest of the days were ironing ... the men used to wear starched collars ... they used a lot of starch 'cos all the aprons from these big houses that the maids wore, they all had to be starched, and the little caps and collars, they were all starched. And the frills had to be 'goffered' with the goffering irons.

Jessie Wilson (born 1911)

The staff of the Ambleside Co-Op in the 1930s. John Ellis is standing on the right.

Ironing at Horrax laundry, Ambleside, mid-1920s.

Packing laundry baskets at Horrax laundry, Ambleside, mid-1920s.

> *Women also worked on farms, in shops, hotels and the post office or as teachers or dressmakers.*

My job was stirring the blood

Me husband and me father did the pig killing. My job at pig killing day was making mulled beer, and stirring the blood when they stuck it you know. And then there were black puddings to make next day, and sausages. Well to tell you the truth, it was me that learned me husband how to cut a pig up.

Mary Birkett (born 1906)

I wanted to do dressmaking

I wanted to do dressmaking, so I started at Madame Jenkinsons for two shillings a week. There were fourteen of us. We'd a good time. She was a good person to work for. I started at 7.30 in the morning, had half an hour for me dinner and finished at 5 o'clock in the evening and never had a Saturday afternoon. We used to sew for lots of people. I was one of the two youngest apprentices and we had our bikes and had to deliver the dresses … it was mostly evening dresses in those days. Even in 1914 we had electric but very poor … this stove stood in the middle to keep the flat iron on for pressing everything.

Anon. (born 1900)

It was very slow work, getting through the snow

I got a job working at Hawkshead post office as a post girl. That was the year of the very deep snow in 1946/47 and I did the village on foot. I went up to Hawkshead Hill, through Shadow Wood and then I walked around as far as Sawrey Ground and then down to Borwick Ground and continued on to Sandground and then back to the village. Then, when it was really very bad, my father decided he would help me because it was very slow work, getting through the snow. He used to whistle so that people would know him, that he was coming and that he didn't frighten them, and he got the nickname of 'The Whistling Postman'.

Dad bought Ionian House in Ambleside in 1950 and we moved there. John took a job on for postman, higher grade. I just wanted to do Bed & Breakfast but my Dad said that if I did, I would get people who weren't married and he didn't want me to have that kind of establishment. So I was all day in the kitchen, making breakfast, packing lunches. I could take seven people there and if they wanted to go out with a packed lunch, I would make them sandwiches and if they wanted to stay in, I made them cold meat and salad and sweet, of course. Then in the evening, it would be soup and the main course, meat and two veg and then pudding … all that for fifteen shillings and sixpence a day. Dogs were welcome as well as children.

Betty Ingham (born 1926)

> *Visitors to the Lake District wanted a vartiety of outdoor activities, and local people were able to start new businesses which catered for them.*

You could catch a bucketful of perch

Wakes week used to be very busy for my father, what with the steamers and the rowing boats. The Lancashire mill workers used to come by rail to Lakeside for days out with their families, which they could get very cheap, and sail the full length of the lake, or take a boat out all day and go fishing. The fish in the lake were very plentiful in those days and if you wanted to you could catch a bucketful of perch, and these were easy for the little children to catch.

William Kellett (born 1902)

We could teach people waterskiing

We started with one boat. I never took on very much more than the one boat at the time. But we started then to waterski and then I found quite a few people who'd like to have a go at waterskiing and one thing and another, so I advertised at the hotel that we could teach people waterskiing and it opened up quite a few doors. I had Richard Dimbleby's two boys, David and Jonathan, and they came up and had a lovely sort of holiday. We taught them both to waterski.

David Scott (born 1923)

> *Life for the men who worked in slate quarries and mines was tough. Earning a living wage was hard.*

We used to live on the job

At Honister slate quarry we used to live on the job; you'd take your food up for the week and you'd start work at seven thirty in the morning and work till four thirty in the afternoon. Then you used to come down and had to start cooking in the barracks, as they called them.

Arnold Lewis (born 1912)

We'd hardly grind our teeth in case we made a spark

When we started at the quarry, at the Old Man of Coniston, serving your time, you learnt about handling the gunpowder. It came in little barrels by horse and cart. And the farmer who carted the slate would bring the gunpowder up and it was in beautiful little barrels, fastened with hazelwood, no nails. Inside was a linen bag and that was tied up. Then we had to carry the barrels into the powder house and you had to put big, leather slippers on to fit over your clogs so that you didn't make a spark. We'd hardly grind our teeth in case we made a spark.

Tommy Robinson (born 1910)

There were no helmets or any protective clothing

I started at Greenside [Glenridding] in 1937 … you used to have a tin full of carbide to fill your lamp up each day. In those days there were no helmets or any protective clothing, you just wore this tweed cap and you had this walking stick because you had to go into this lead mine. You had to walk along the rails, the rails the loco ran on. A lot of water from the upper workings were continually flowing down through the Lucy level … you had to walk a mile before you came to the shaft. The Moors shaft took you down to 175 fathoms. It was a very dangerous job. You used to drill and fire and then you'd have this huge cavity. You had to know exactly where to drill and how much explosive to use … shatter the rock and it becomes dangerous … this big stone fell and killed a man.

Arnold Lewis (born 1912)

If they made nowt they got nowt

They'd very little overhead expenses see, just their explosives and tool sharpening and such like, 'cos a lot of that stuff could be worked out by hand you see. Colthowe was a different seam altogether to Spout Crag. Spout Crag is much rougher. Colthowe is fine slate, and get back on't bank here and there's fine slate there but they always bothered with rushing you see. Folk in them days got what they worked for, if they made nowt they got nowt.

Braithwaite Rigg (born 1903)

Tommy Robinson, quarryman.

Lake District bed and breakfast landladies in the 1950s.

> *In the past, when health and safety were not high priorities, accidents at work were unfortunately all too common.*

I got a post driven through my tummy

At Horrax's bobbin mill I got a post driven right through my tummy off a circular saw. I lived in hospital for about six years ... and I had a finger off as well from a circular saw and I nearly cut my thumb off.

Cecil Otway (born 1910)

It was like a battlefield up there

Accidents did happen [in the lead mines] and a bad day was 7th of July 1952. You see you often got gas, carbon monoxide gas after you'd fired, when the smoke would hang about and you often got a thick head. Now the whole shift started walking up the north end [of Greenside mine, Glenridding] and they met this gas so they started back ... a man had gone down in a sort of bucket and he got to the bottom and shouted to be pulled up but when the hoist man tried to pull him up there was no air so he couldn't. They had no rescue team ... it was like a battlefield up there. I was not allowed to go back into the mine as it was too dangerous. Men from West Cumberland came and tried to get the men out and they had to search the mine that night, but they never got down to them for ten days and they had a big funeral for them in Patterdale, a military funeral because they were mostly ex-servicemen, and the Bishop of Carlisle took the service. It was dreadful.

Arnold Lewis, Greenside lead mine (born 1912)

The main chain snapped and wrapped round his leg

My husband fetched about £12 a week home quarrying and he used to work right down in the hole at Hodge Close slate quarry. He used to go down a little iron ladder in the side of the rock face, and there was a ledge of about 8 or 10 yards wide, and there was a drop of about 150ft of water that had been excavated earlier. Off this ledge were several tunnels into the rock. They were pulling a great big chunk out on chains, the chains were dragging along the ground, and my husband was guiding it out when the main chain snapped and wrapped itself round his leg and threw him down ... they couldn't get a doctor to go down and it was three and a half hours before they got him out. They didn't think they could save his leg. We had industrial injury money with him not working of £5 1s and I never owed a penny. He went back into hospital eight times through the next fifteen months.

Anon. (born 1934)

Many men worked in the woods and the timber they produced was used for a wide variety of products. Forestry in the 1960s was still largely unmechanised.

We would be three days on a tree

We used just 7lb felling axes to fell a tree together with a cross-cut saw. Everybody was vying with each other to be an expert with a 7lb pine axe – I was one of them. I rather fancied myself with it. I could do quite well with a felling axe but it was very hard work, good exercise. It usually took about a day for two chaps to get a tree ready to cut down with a cross-cut saw. We would be three days on a tree. We used horses in the inaccessible slopes, because the ordinary basic tractor only goes so far up a steep slope. In 1966 we got our first four-wheel drive tractor and we had an experiment with it on Claife. I actually drove it up this wood on the steep side of Claife. It was absolutely amazing; you couldn't do that with an ordinary tractor.

Ken Parker (born 1931)

Forestry work at Claife.

Farming in the Lake District was the mainstay of life for generations of local families, and farmhands found jobs at hiring fairs, which were held twice-yearly in Cockermouth, Carlisle, Penrith, Ulverston and Barrow. Farmhands and girls lived in, and though wages were low, food was generally plentiful.

They gave you a shilling

You'd just stand away, then the farmer would come up and say, 'Hello, are you looking for a job or have you got a spot?' And you'd get to work talking, and you'd say, 'No, no, I'm looking for a spot.' 'Aye, what can you do? Can you milk, can you use a lay, can you work a horse?' Then you'd start bartering about price, but you never got very far away with them.

Harry Wilson (born 1908)

There was a share and a bottle for every man

Start six o'clock in the morning. You could hear the old man coming down, there was nine of us hired there: 'Come on, me lads, its going to be neet before we get started.' It was nobbut six o'clock, and then we had all to milk, clean out and fodder up and then in for breakfast – a bowl of porridge, a big bowl, and then summertime there was a bowl of new milk on the table and you got a basin-full of that, and you had some bread and cheese, and on the end of the table there was a share and a bottle for every man; that was your ten o'clocks, you took that out with you.

Isaac Greenhow (born 1902)

The farmer's wife looked after you

We used to take all our things in what they called a tin box with our clothing in, aye … and on't farm, the farmer's wife looked after you – mending your socks and washing your clothes.

Stan Wilson (born 1907)

A lowland valley farm might grow potatoes, turnips, grass for hay, corn, wheat and oats; the turnips had to be sown and set up, then weeded, and the thistles had to be mowed out of the pasture fields before anyone started on hay-timing; after that the corn was ready to be harvested, followed by the potatoes and then the stubble would be ready for ploughing. There was milking to be done twice daily, the animals fed, lambing both night and day, and all the young stock to be cared for. There was never a dull moment: clipping, dipping, going to market, or training a new sheepdog or draught horse. Despite the short growing season, many farms grew their own corn which was threshed in the farm's own horse gin.

The old horses knew us

We used to thresh our own corn. We had one of those rings; they called them a gin ring, where you drove the horse round and round. That was our job, the girls could drive the horse, then inside the machinery you put the sheaves and it threshed them and separated the corn and the chaff and we used to hate it. You got so tired going round and round, 'cos the old horses knew us, and they wouldn't go on.

Sally Bulman (born 1896)

> *Upland farms were mostly restricted to sheep and cattle, although oats and turnips were also grown for winter feed.*

We'd make butter in them days

We had a farm called Sunny Brow, mainly sheep and a few cows. We'd make butter in them days. We didn't sell any milk. It was all separated and cream made into butter … my mother did that. Father was on his own. No hired labour. He used to work together with some of t'neighbours. We used to plough quite a bit. I've ploughed many an acre with horses in my time. We had at least two working horses – Clydesdales. Then he used to breed a few. We grew oats. First year we plough up it was oats, next year it was turnips and potatoes and then oats again the third year, and so on down with grass seed at the same time. That was all winter feed for the stock. We always made enough hay, mowed with a horse machine. We'd move on with machine to the next farm, and work together in that way.

Isaac Witwell (born 1902)

> *While horses played such an important role in farming and forestry, every community had a blacksmith.*

I often used to pump up the forge

There was the blacksmith's shop at Town End, Grasmere, and the blacksmith was known as Roydy Walker. He was still there when I was a lad, was Roydy Walker, because I often used to pump up the forge for him, put my hand on the old pump and pump away with the bellows and I was intrigued watching him fashioning horseshoes and other things.

David Scott (born 1923)

> *The arrival of tractors in the 1940s heralded the mechanisation of farming, and fewer jobs for farmhands.*

There was hundreds and hundreds on a train

Our first tractor was a Ford. It had a great big iron seat and the clutch and the brake were all in one so when you put the clutch in it went faster before you could put the brake on. It didn't slow down! The next one, in the 1950s, would be a Massey Ferguson – a little grey Fergie. I always remember them coming into Milnthorpe station and they would put them into the sidings, these Massey Fergies and there was hundreds and hundreds on a train.

Malcolm Parsons (born 1947)

Eskdale, Cumberland, September 1924. Rain day after day does not promise well for the prospect of harvesting fine crops of corn, but the Lake District farmers are doing their best. (Courtesy CWAAS/Mary Fell Collection)

Blacksmith Fred Satterthwaite working in the family smithy at Belle Green, Sawrey, assisted by his cousin George Devon during the 1930s. Beatrix Potter lodged at the smithy with Fred's mother, Harriet Satterthwaite, just before she moved in to Castle Cottage.

A 'little grey Fergie' tractor: Massey Ferguson Model TE20 manufactured between 1946 and 1956.

> *From the 1930s there have been other opportunities for employment associated with specialist facilities for science and the arts. The Freshwater Biological Association's laboratories at Ferry House on the shore of Windermere have been responsible for pioneering research in many branches of science. This included the analysis of pollen changes in the lake sediments, which has had considerable significance for the understanding of past climate and vegetation patterns.*

You can see the era of atom bomb testing

One of the biggest things that the Freshwater Biological Association ever did was research into the history of lakes since the Ice Age. After the Ice Age, you have clays deposited on the lake bed with layers, exactly like the rings of a tree, each layer represents the yearly deposition. What gave the clues were the nature of the material – the pollen and the diatoms – which came into the lakes, which varied according to what was going on in the landscape and in the water.

On top of that you can do other things, you can do the actual chemistry of the mud. John Mackereth was a most extraordinary man and he invented a 'corer', which took much better cores than earlier versions and he found a magnetic method of measuring time in the cores. You can see the era of atom bomb testing and then the agreement to stop testing; you can measure the whole thing in the core and you can date it. You can even pick up the Chernobyl stuff.

John Lund (born 1912)

The Mackereth corer emerging from Lake Windermere. (© David Livingstone, Freshwater Biological Association)

> *The promotion of Wordsworth's connections to Grasmere initially by the Dove Cottage Trust, and more recently by the Wordsworth Trust, has created a leading centre for the study of the Romantic movement. This has brought many poets and scholars to work in the Lake District.*

The British Centre for Romanticism

About 1970 Robert [Woof] became a trustee of the Wordsworth Trust, and when in 1992 he became director he managed to raise money for resident poets and for poetry readings. And they have continued to the present day. Robert believed and the trustees believe that there is a very fruitful interchange between the poetry of the past and the poetry of the present. He also

dealt, as it were, with Dove Cottage as a building, inviting architects to help make it suitable for tens of thousands of visitors. He was also able to buy the coachhouse of the Prince of Wales Hotel, and convert it into a museum and the museum opened in 1982, and that became the show place for our manuscripts.

Sometimes Robert used to say the centre ought to be called the British Centre for Romanticism. He did have that vision that Wordsworth was not alone as a poet. He lived in a world with other poets, and he lived in a context, historically. So what Robert wanted to preserve was not only Wordsworth but the manuscripts of the people he read, of people whom he influenced.

Pamela Woof (born 1931)

Dr Robert Woof (on the right) with Seamus Heaney at the opening of the Jerwood Centre for the Wordsworth Trust, Grasmere, 2005. (Courtesy of The Wordsworth Trust)

> *Mechanisation reduced the numbers working in farming and quarries but tourism and the leisure industry provided a wealth of new jobs. However, the Lake District now strives to diversify, having become over-dependent on tourism in a fluctuating economy. Success stories abound – slate is quarried and exported worldwide for building work, and other firms which originated in the Lake District during the past fifty years have become household names and opened high street branches throughout the UK, with their headquarters still in Cumbria. Locally produced specialist food products are also appearing on the UK's supermarket shelves, and the wool from the backs of the hardy Herdwick ewes are now used as insulation and in making carpets.*

seven

SPORTS

The Lake District may not be known for its Premier League football clubs or county cricket, but the area probably hosts as wide a variety of sporting activities as anywhere in the country. Sport was part of the fabric of the community and the oldest and most popular sporting traditions continued to be those which sprang from the surrounding fells and valleys, such as hunting on foot, fell running and hound trailing (a race for hounds). The village sportsdays included traditional flat races, but the centrepieces were the fell or 'guide' races and the unique Cumberland and Westmorland wrestling. Most Lake District sports were originally for men, but women now compete in track events, as well as fell running and wrestling.

> *Coniston Foxhounds was founded in 1825 to provide sport, but hunting was later looked on as a necessity.*

In those days we killed about forty foxes a year

When I started [1944] the foxes weren't as numerous by a long way to what they are now, they were not. Say you went into Rydal Park, we'd only perhaps find one fox and away it would go, it would land about Helvellyn. In those days we killed about forty foxes a year, but now [in the 1980s] between seventy and eighty. It's as I say, there were more people after them in them days. In those days keepers would be trapping and shooting, but these traps, they've been done away with now.

Anthony Chapman, Huntsman, Coniston Foxhounds (born 1914)

> *The Huntsman was responsible for the daily care of the hounds.*

Everything was on foot

I came in on a bike. That's what I had. A bike. From Rydal on a bike. There were nae motor cars … you know I used to walk from here everywhere, once upon a time. I used to walk from these kennels to Coniston, Strawberry Bank, Cartmel Fell, High Newton, Woodland, with the pack.

Coniston
Foxhounds at
Rydal, 1920s.

Everything was on foot, yes. That was when nearly all the gamekeepers were done away with during the war, people couldn't afford to keep them, they nivver came back, only at the odd houses.

Anthony Chapman, Huntsman, Coniston Foxhounds (born 1914)

The special trail rags were like woollen rags, soaked in paraffin and aniseed

For the standard trail we'd to go to Rydal Head. We'd to walk up there and then there were two persons, one each way, and we'd to climb up onto the fell then come back in and down through Nab Scar, one side or the other, came down through Rydal. The main trail was about five miles. The special trail rags were like woollen rags, soaked in paraffin and aniseed, mixed. It had to be specially done by the Hound Trail Association, you see, because it was a special mixture. You couldn't just mix your own.

Harry Mawson (born 1913)

Flat racing, fell racing and Cumberland and Westmorland wrestling took place at Ambleside and Grasmere Sports, and still do.

There was three or four fell races (Ambleside Sports)

There was flat racing, 100 metres and 200 or 300 metres race round the ring with children. At one time they were very good, was the children. We used to get them from West Cumberland. There was three or four fell races – up what they call High Pike, up Scandale.

Harry Mawson (born 1913)

It's all what we call 'in the knack'

It was just the local sport, you know, the farmers and the farm workers and all that used to congregate on the village greens. Families got together, it was like a big family gathering. Our family always came back for Grasmere Sports day. They used to wrestle – to get a pair, they used to throw their hats in and there was two hats picked up and those two wrestled, you see. That's how it originated.

In the 150 year history of Grasmere Sports, wrestling was in it the whole time. We've championships at various weights and competitions at various weights but originally, when it first started, you'd your eight and a half stones up to your heavyweights. But now the lightest weight we wrestle for is ten stones, the under eighteens; then we've the heavyweights at various weights.

It'd be in our teens we'd start, because travelling was a difficulty for us, you see. It wasn't until we got a motorcycle of our own that we travelled away for competitions. My brother was one of the top wrestlers. The actual technique of the wrestling is different. Your back-holds, you see, one arm under and one arm over and you take a back hold and then you've different chips, which you apply with the rest of your body – your feet, your legs or whatever, which we call 'chips' you see. You get your outside arms, your inside arms, your leg up buttocks, your full buttocks, your cross buttocks, and then you've got your defences you see. A good wrestler is a good defensive wrestler. He knows his move, he knows his man's coming and you go against that, you see … he counteracts it, you see … Sometimes you can throw your opponent off the chip that he's coming with. It's all what we call 'in the knack'. What constitutes a win? The first man that hits the ground with any part of his body above the knee. During the winter time they're training young lads – well, we do it at the Leisure Centre at Kendal and Waberthwaite and Bootle, they have wrestling academies there.

Thomas Mason (born 1931)

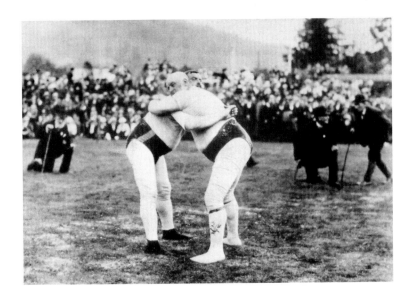

Traditional wrestling at Grasmere sports, 1900s.

> *Fell running in the twenty-first century is also as popular as ever.*

Everybody buggers off into the mist for four hours

Most of the amateur competitors ran Fairfield Horseshoe type races, and then the West Coast clubs organised the really long ones at Wasdale and Ennerdale and that's about all there was originally. They race nearly up every hill in the Lake District now, at one time or another. Well, locally I've done all the Coniston, Fairfield, Skiddaw, all the Keswick ones, done the really long ones, Borrowdale, Wasdale, Ennerdale – which takes four or five hours to get round. I think you get an 'elite' certificate if you beat four hours on Ennerdale ... I remember one time a journalist came up to cover the races, I think from the *Guardian*, he asked the organisers, 'What goes on at these fell races?' And they said, 'Well, everybody buggers off into the mist for four hours and comes back again and that's about it, really!' They're really tough, those. I notice now that these sort of races are petering out and the shorter races are much more well supported. Ten years ago, there were 200 running the Ennerdale, but it's all changing. There's a lot of difference between my generation and modern, where you did a lot of hill walking, a lot of time on the hills generally; you developed a mountain sense. Nowadays you're getting people who are fast road runners coming in that are very, very good athletes but there's no navigational skill required at all. It's just blindly following the person in front of you. It only needs the mist to come down and it will totally disorientate you on the top of Fairfield and you finish up down in Glenridding.

Geoff Clayton (born 1947)

> *Football was, and is, universally popular wherever there is an open space.*

It was a case of make do and mend

We used to always play football of course, but we didn't always have a football. If we had an old tennis ball, we would kick that about for ages; if we couldn't find a ball, we would get newspaper, roll it up into a big ball, as big as we could get, tie it round with string to make it really tight and kick that about until it dropped to pieces. If we could borrow a football from anybody, it would be an advantage but it wasn't always possible. It was a case of make do and mend.

John Ellis (born 1910)

Geoff Clayton fell running.

Most villages had football, rugby and cricket teams. Cricket and rugby appealed initially to those who were public or grammar school educated.

The famous Bell family were all giants

Ambleside Cricket Club was started by the wealthy people from the big houses and they'd only play cricket in July and August I think, when they broke up at public schools and universities. The Squire of Rydal, and also the Redmaynes of Brathay Hall, played cricket for Ambleside: they were quite good cricketers. The rugby would start similar, but rugby very quickly took in local people like the Bells – the five Bell brothers who played rugby … the famous Bell family of Bells chemists were all giants.

William Thornborough (born 1919)

As tourism expanded at the end of the nineteenth century, people began to use the landscape for a variety of new sports, rather than just looking at the scenery. Both summer and winter provided excellent opportunities, though with few winter visitors, sports such as sledging, skating and skiing were until more recently dominated by local people.

Fell walking as a pastime became popular with the influx of wealthy families and growing numbers of holidaymakers, most arriving by train. More specialised activities such as rock climbing and fell running developed alongside the enthusiasm for fell walking. The lakes also became a focus for a range of water sports, including rowing and yachting. Waterskiing had to await the arrival of speedboats between the wars, but has recently and controversially been curtailed on the lakes by a 10mph speed limit.

Sports such as golf, tennis and sailing appealed to both sexes.

There used to be a golf course up on Loughrigg Fell

I played golf on Loughrigg. There used to be a golf course up there, up on Loughrigg Fell. It had nine, very difficult – I think the second one was about three or four feet from a wall and the other side were rocks, so if the ball hit the rocks, it came back to you.

Vera Bunting (born 1920)

I can remember the umpire's chair

I remember the Westmorland Tennis Tournament which used to take place – the most beautiful tennis courts at the Rothay Hotel [Grasmere] at the back, in the grounds there … I can remember the umpire's chair, him sitting up in the chair and the tennis going on and the waitresses coming out of the hotel with great big silver trays covered in teacakes and scones.

Joyce Withers (born 1934)

> *Yachting was the sport of the rich families who lived around the lakes, many of whom owned their own yacht.*

She was a very pleasant boat to sail

If the weather was fine, we spent an awful lot of time either down by the lake or in boats. We had three rowing boats, a dinghy and a large sailing yacht called *Mañana*, which was gaff-rigged and had at one time an enormous amount of canvas. One of my uncles was very nervous and he kept having some of the canvas removed from *Mañana*, so she got slower and slower but she was a very pleasant boat to sail and, funnily enough, is still in the Steamboat Museum at Bowness.

Charmian Piper, Wanlass Howe (born 1923)

> *Early waterskiing on Windermere was a very primitive affair.*

It was the old-fashioned way of waterskiing, on a board

It was the Ambleside/Waterhead Carnival, which was about 1924, and it was always very cold you know, and it was rather new to be towed behind a motorboat in those days. Of course it's nothing like they do now, holding on to ropes. Well [William] Heaton Cooper, the young son of the artist Alfred Heaton Cooper – he wanted to try and he was very plucky really. It was a very cold day, and he was going along quite well, and then he fell off, and nobody took much notice 'cos they thought he'd come up again; and he came sort of half up, and then went down again. And my brother, who was in the boat, realised what was happening and went straight over the side with his hat on and his shoes, and mackintosh and everything, and found Heaton, who was very nearly drowned. It was the old-fashioned

Above: Harry Martin waterskiing on Windermere in the 1920s.

Right: Cissy Penrice and Joan Martin at White Platts, 1946.

way of waterskiing, on a board, you know, with the rope and rather a slow motorboat sort of chugging along.

Alison Carrington-Smith (born 1909) and Barbara McKechnie (born 1913)

> *The lakes and fells in winter provided an ideal playground for sledging, skating and skiing.*

We used to get our trays

It was all just fields. We used to wander up Oaksfield in winter when we had the snows. We used to get our trays, not so much sledges, we used to have trays, a biggish tray. And we used to get on at the top and come down to the bottom of Oaksfield sledging. We had some wonderful times.

Peggy Langdon (born 1922)

Skating with his hands behind his back

In 1929 Rydal Lake was frozen for weeks. I spent a lot of time down there in the ghastly skates that you sort of strapped on to your rather ill-fitting boots, and somehow you managed to skate. It was just local people, there just weren't visitors in the wintertime. Nobody went on the ice until Mr Mason tested it. I remember him skating on the ice all by himself with his hands behind his back with a long swinging stride. Once he had said it was alright, we were allowed to go on.

Anne Beddard (born 1920)

They had a wind-up gramophone which played the Skaters' Waltz

In the 1940s White Moss Tarn was an excellent stretch of ice for skating on. I was given a pair of adjustable, screw-on skates and I made my first attempt to learn to skate and someone gave me a small chair to push over the ice and I began to make a little bit of headway in learning to skate by that means. I can remember seeing people skating up there in the moonlight, which is absolutely wonderful, really. I particularly remember an old couple who were really superb skaters. They had a wind-up gramophone which played the Skaters' Waltz.

Derek Setford (born 1936)

We plodded up on skins up to Sticks Pass

After the Second World War there was a very flourishing Lake District Ski Club. We used to have weekend meets on Raise and we plodded up on skins up to Sticks Pass from Thirlspot or up to Greenside Mines from Glenridding, how useful those skins were. And there was a little hut built by members on Raise, where we could have our hot soup and gather when the weather became too nasty, and also a small, petrol-driven mobile ski lift was put up there

Major Porter skating at Rydal Water, 1926.

by some of the enthusiastic members. We had a lot of members from the Penrith area who did a great deal for the club in those days. I remember some brilliant, absolutely brilliant days looking at Stybarrow Dodd and perhaps going up on Stybarrow Dodd and making one's own tracks down. Days that you just never forget and other days that you remember for different reasons – when you could just barely see other skiers come out of the mist.

Joan Whitworth (born 1918)

> *Rock climbing began largely as the visiting sport of a young, university-educated elite, but was soon taken up by local lads such as Jim Birkett and Sid Cross. Great Gable was a favourite destination.*

We climbed the Needles with our coffin rope

Soon we took a rope with us, one that Charlie had got out of his father's garage, and it was the rope his father had used for lowering coffins into graves. And he pinched that, and we went over to the Napes to climb the Needles [on Great Gable], and we climbed the Needles with our coffin rope. We wore galoshes. Climbing cost practically nothing because we'd no money. A pair of galoshes cost 1s 11d. We saved up for a rope, and this rope was a beer rope and cost 11s 9d for 80 foot, and off we went to Pavey Ark.

Sid Cross (born 1913)

Skating on Rydal Water, 1945.

Left: Jim Birkett belayed by Charlie Wilson on Kern Knotts, Great Gable, on a direct variation of his route to Kern Knotts Crack. The rope is hemp tied with a bowline around his waist and he is wearing nailed boots.(© Bill Birkett Photo Library, www.billbirkett.co.uk)

Right: Single file over the packhorse bridge at Watendlath. (Courtesy of Cumbria County Council, Kendal Library)

Left: St John Ambulance volunteers on a crag rescue exercise in the 1930s.

> *A few women joined in, sometimes with their boyfriends.*

I used to wear men's trousers

The boyfriend that I had in those days climbed with a group of men. I think I was welcome, but when they stopped at a pub on the way home to have a glass of beer, I had to sit outside! We cycled from Kendal of course to Langdale, or to Coniston, and then climbed all day, and I'd cycle back at night. In the 1920s I used to wear men's trousers. Yes trousers. You couldn't climb without them could you?

Jammie Cross (born 1912)

> *Fell walking was popularised by the 1930s fashion for hiking, and the growth of youth hostel accommodation.*

The bus went at 10 o'clock and it was usually packed

We just had jumpers and skirts and flat shoes but after a few years I got a pair of boots. We also had like an anorak, which wasn't like they are today – very thin, and I always had a sou'wester, a yellow sou'wester. We usually went on the bus and if we went up Langdale way, the bus always went at 10 o'clock in the morning and it was usually packed – standing, it was. Crowds of people on it, mostly visitors, not many locals. You used to have to queue up to get on the bus. Maybe we'd go up Rossett Ghyll onto Great End and sit up there for the day and then come back the same way. Sometimes we'd go up The Band and up Bowfell and then round onto Esk Hause and down Rossett Ghyll …

Vera Bunting (born 1920)

They used to ride ponies

Very often walkers used to come during the year to see the sun rise above Scafell. They set off at midnight. They used to want strong black coffee before they set off. They always went to Scafell to see that. The women folk, they used to ride the ponies up to Esk Hause. And they used to go up the Pikes as well – that's the pony track.

Frank and Margaret Birkett (both born 1902)

> *With increasing numbers of climbers and walkers, more mishaps occurred, but it wasn't until the late 1940s that mountain rescue became organised. Before that time St John Ambulance volunteers joined forces with local police and farmers to rescue anyone injured or lost. Using farmers' rope and old gates for stretchers, men went out with hurricane lamps to bring down the injured. Many Langdale rescues were carried out from the Old Dungeon Ghyll Hotel, which was run by Sid Cross.*

Sid Cross, pioneer mountain-rescuer.

A cliff rescue exercise, 1975.

When I looked down it was Calor Gas Ernie

I remember an occasion when this fellow had broken one leg and an ankle on Middle Fell Buttress – high up. And there was no one about, no one at all. We formed this little Langdale team of Gerald, who was working for us and was a student and a climber, and another lad that was working for us, a student but non-climber, and me. So there were only three of us went out to get this fellow off Middle Fell Buttress and we got up to him, stretcher and everything. I banged two lots of morphia into him, he was in such a bad state, and then fit up the belays, and Gerald and the other lad were lowering me down and a voice said, 'OK Sid, I'll help you,' and when I looked down it was Calor Gas Ernie – Ernie Rigg, who used to take the Calor Gas round, who was not a mountaineer or a climber, had seen that there was a need, and he'd gone up there, up the gully. These are the things that have been such a pleasure.

Sid Cross (born 1913)

Since those early years of mountain rescue, teams all over the Lake District established themselves as highly-trained life savers supported by RAF helicopters and air ambulances, adapting the latest in technology to make mountain rescue the highly specialised voluntary service it is proud to be. The sporting activities of the twenty-first century have become a blend of traditional Lake District sports, national sports and outdoor pursuits for which the region is internationally known.

eight

ENTERTAINMENT

In the past the world of entertainment was very different from that of today. Entertainment was often spontaneous or organised within families, and given the natural environment of the Lake District, young and old enjoyed the opportunities provided in the landscape. Communities came together to celebrate events and entertain themselves, and a surprising variety of travelling entertainers also visited, though they were not necessarily always of a high standard.

At the centre of many villages was the Reading Room or Institute, sometimes given by the squire or local landowner, while others were built by public subscription. Their primary purpose was to enable the local population, mainly the men, to improve themselves through education. The rooms always included a library with newspapers, and they were also used for classes and lectures. Tables and chairs were provided, but otherwise they were pretty spartan. In the smaller villages the Institute was often the only space that could hold a gathering of people, so they were also the venue for social events.

The *Daily Dispatch* was provided for you to read

The Institute, we used to call it the Reading Room, had the daily papers and the local paper and the *Daily Dispatch* was provided for you to read, and there was one at Brathay, and there was one at Wray and there was one at Sawrey. All these little villages had their Institute or Reading Room … The only time I ever remember women going into the Reading Room was when they used to have dances there and my mother used to play the piano … four or five hefty lads would carry the piano from my grandmother's house and then there'd be a dance or a sports night or a wedding.

Len Crossley (born 1915)

There used to be some good do's

In the Reading Room at Rydal there was a Bagatelle table and a few card tables, and there used to be some good do's in there. We used to have little concerts and all sorts of things, even dances … but there was no beer, oh no.

Margaret Greenup (born 1895)

Everybody had a bit of a party piece

In the winter time they'd social evenings, a bit of everything; you'd intermittent dances, and people singing and reciting. Social evenings were going on the whole time; most organisations ran them, the YMCA, the Conservative Club. You'd go, and there'd be a band there, somebody would play on the piano or an accordion and there'd be a bit of a dance. They'd have a dance or two and after a bit they'd stop and then somebody would do a bit of singing, or a comedian, all that sort, and then a few more dances and then there'd be a bit of a bun fight, tea in the interval and then somebody reciting dialect, a bit more singing or a conjuror. Everybody had a bit of a party piece, and these do's would start about eight and finish about eleven. They were regular all through the winter at places like Rydal Reading Room.

William Thornborough (born 1919)

Everybody went with gloves and hats

The Grasmere Citizens Association used to meet in Grasmere Hall about once a month, under the sponsorship of Mrs Rawnsley. And they had a lecturer, they had light refreshments and then they had a dance – and it wasn't a barn dance, it was a dance. And it was very carefully supervised by Mrs Rawnsley to make sure that the young people didn't misbehave in any way. And everybody went with gloves and hats … it was all terribly prim and proper.

Joyce Cockcroft (born 1917)

> *Communities created their own entertainments. Grasmere was especially renowned during the 1920s and '30s for its dialect plays. People came by the coachload to Grasmere to see the dialect play each February.*

They were written about local characters

They were famous in their day, and quite amusing; they're very simple, but they had fabulous settings, really beautiful settings … they were written about local characters, local situations, in local dialect. They were village stories, really, a bit like *The Archers*, just stories of village life.

Joyce Cockcroft (born 1917)

The Rydal Reading Room.

A scene from one of the Grasmere Dialect Plays. (Courtesy of The Wordsworth Trust)

A popular entertainment in Ambleside was the tableau, created to mark any big occasion such as Christmas, May Day, a coronation or a jubilee. Some were extremely elaborate using hired costumes, and mostly owed their popularity to the enthusiasm of just three or four ladies in Ambleside during the 1930s. One May Day, instead of the normal crowning festivities, there was a Miss Coronation tableau to mark the Coronation of George VI. Several girls, all aged twenty-five, were sought to make up the crown, with rubies, sapphires and ermine all around. But at the last moment the top part of the crown was missing and a gold lamé dress failed to arrive from a Kendal dressmaker.

Half an hour before I should have gone on, the dress hadn't come

I had to have my dress made myself and it had to have a train, so I chose a wedding dress. We had it made in gold lamé … well, it never came. And half an hour before I should have gone on the dress hadn't come. Mr Hayes had to rush in his car and go to the shop, which was closed, find out where the dressmaker lived, rush her to the shop, and bring the dress. The performance was held up until I got there. Everybody was in a flat spin but I wasn't a bit bothered. Of course it could have spoiled it. I was the main piece of the crown. It never bothered me, and then when I got on the top of this table I had to sing 'Land of Hope and Glory'. Goodness, what I remember about those marvellous nights! They really were. There was another May Day tableau, St George and the Dragon, and I sent to a firm in Liverpool for my outfit … it had a visor, a sword and everything.

Mary Hallatsch (born 1912)

Ambleside May Queen festivities, with Mary Hallatsch as the jewel in the crown, George VI Coronation Tableau, 1937.

Musical events were always popular both for the performers and the audience. Operas brought people from all walks of life together as the only criterion for participating was that you should have a good singing voice.

Fancy having operas in Ambleside

In Ambleside they had operas. When you think about it, fancy having operas in Ambleside, and they were mostly locals in it. Even the man I worked for, Arthur Jackson, his wife and daughter were in the opera, and my late wife's brother was in the opera. They were all in the opera.

Alan Capstick (born 1910)

They plugged away at it

One old bandsman told me that whatever the opera was going to do next, they would practise it all winter and the next summer, wherever they went to – galas, sports … whatever opera they were doing they played all that music and they plugged away at it into people's minds so by the time the opera came round, they were all wanting to see it and they knew all the tunes inside out.

John Inman (born 1912)

> *Dances, which were held anywhere where there was a suitable space, were especially popular in the villages between the wars.*

We really looked forward to it

There were dances in the school, they'd have a dance. There was a fiddle, a cornet, tambourine – no fancy band. There was the polka and the waltz, and the barn dances. The Quadrilles are eightsomes, and the same for the Lancers. Everybody put their heart and soul into it you see. They only had it twice a year so we really looked forward to it.

May Bowness (born 1901)

A real session in them days

Our main entertainment was going to the Hunt Ball, but then they used to last 'til three in the morning, we used to have a real session in them days with a knife and fork supper.

Albert Bowness (born 1907)

> *There were several formal balls held each winter at Ambleside Assembly Rooms. Good behaviour was expected, and although anyone that could afford the price of a ticket could go, people gravitated towards members of their own social class.*

Between the wars we had some balls

Between the wars we had some balls. We thought they were fabulous, and still everyone was dressed in a suit to start with, and most of the men had dancing shoes, these glossy shoes. They'd also got a good band or orchestra. But a lot of MCs were terribly strict. They wouldn't allow anyone to take drink in. They used to search people and if anybody was a bit unsteady they used to turn 'em out!

William Thornborough (born 1919)

There were three classes of people

There was the Conservative Ball, the Liberals, the Boys Brigade, and the Fire Brigade in the Assembly Rooms … and the room below was all beautifully decorated and great long trestle tables done out with flowers and everything. It was very funny, there were three classes of people at these dances, there was probably the Redmaynes, and those from places like Loughrigg Brow all at the very top against the orchestra. And then there was, well, I was amongst them, and my friends and farmers and such like, then down at the very bottom – I always laugh about it – was what they called the Laundry clique, a lot of girls. The laundry then that Bernard Horrax had, there was a whole lot of them, and they always had the bottom of the floor. They always called them the Laundry clique because they always stuck together down there.

Margaret Greenup (born 1895)

> *People looked forward to local entertainments that travelled around the district.*

The Ragtime Cowboy Joe Show

Old Joe King was a grand one for getting things up; well he got up the Ragtime Cowboy Joe Show; it was marvellous. The stage was covered with all these Indians and that you know, really wonderful, and we always called him Ragtime Cowboy Joe.

Margaret Greenup (born 1895)

Wild West tableau before the First World War.

They corked up their faces

Major Rothwell's Dandy Coons, a troupe of thirty black and white minstrels, used to be sidesmen and bowmen and they used to sing all the negro spiritual songs. They corked up their faces and they had uniforms, red lapels and black buttons. They were chiefly men, and they were got up by Major Rothwell of Broomleas, Esthwaite Water. You could hire them, but they used to come and I don't know if they made any profit but I think they did it more for pleasure really.

Len Crossley (born 1915)

> *The circus came every year.*

It had a big menagerie

In those days in summer, all the circuses used to come touring round the villages, and there was one called Sanders. It had a big menagerie, which was entirely like a big zoo on wheels, and they used to come in the park and set them out in a big square, and you had to pay an entrance to go in and see all these animals, and watch when they put all the lions in one big cage where the lion tamer went in with them. Then there was another called Bill's Wild West Circus and there we used to see 'The attack on the Deadwood Mail', with the coach galloping round and the Indians chasing after it on their horses and there was sort of imitation fire going on inside and the cowboys firing blank cartridges; we lapped it up!

Percy Middleton (born 1904)

> *The silver screen travelled to the villages.*

They used to get a full house

In those days Scotts Cinematograph used to come. There was no picture house then, they used to come with this travelling cinema. They used to get a full house.

Margaret Greenup (born 1895)

There would always be a comic one on the end

We would have a film like *Ivanhoe* and then there would always be a comic one on the end, like Charlie Chaplin or Buster Keaton. There was never anyone selling sweets or anything like that; just to get in, for tuppence-ha' penny, that was the thing.

Percy Middleton (born 1904)

He was very clever at improvising

There was a chap called Wedgewood Turner used to play the piano for the silent films, all this incidental music; the Wild West stuff. He was very clever at improvising and he was wonderful, we thought. It never seemed the same after the talkies, we missed him.

William Thornborough (born 1919)

> *There were so many evening activities that some people rarely spent a night at home.*

You want to take your bed there

I joined Mr Skelton's male voice choir, and then they roped me in for the Choral Society, and then they roped me in for bell ringing, then Hawkshead Male Voice Choir. I was in all three. There was Male Voice Choir on Monday, bell ringing Tuesday, Wednesday night was a free night, Thursday was Choral Society, Friday night was the church choir; and my wife said, 'You want to take your bed there, you're never at home!'

Alfred Creighton (born 1900)

Alfred Creighton still making music on his mouth-organ.

> *The Langdale valley's annual outing to Morecambe was the farthest most lads from Langdale could expect to travel. It was the greatest day of the year for some.*

It was such a great day out

It was the day of the year for the old fellows – they put roses in their buttonholes and got decked up and they were coming down past the forge at five o'clock ready for about half past seven here at Colwith. You know it was such a great day out, you could have taken Little Langdale by storm that day, there was only about three left out of the valley. But the buses had canvas tops and nay sides in and on one occasion we set off from here and conked out at Elterwater. We only got a mile and a half and we conked out!

Albert Bowness (born 1907)

> *Young lads took great pleasure in swimming in lakes. One of the most popular watering spots was at Waterhead, Ambleside, just near the Galava Roman fort where the council even built bathing huts.*

There were three compartments

The bathing huts faced Waterhead and there were three compartments; the attendant's compartment, there was a ladies and a gents, and then there were posts round the back where people could change free of charge – but if they wanted to go in the huts, they'd to pay a little bit. They had a full-time attendant for the season.

William Thornborough (born 1919)

> *Girls enjoyed outdoor activities in Girl Guides, and annual camps were held on land belonging to Beatrix Potter.*

She came out dressed as one of her rabbits

We used to go to Sawrey to camp, and we went to Beatrix Potter's last birthday when we were in Guide Camp, and we all dressed up as characters from her books to go and sing 'Happy Birthday to You' because she just lived in the village … and she came out dressed up as one of her rabbits in a bonnet to show how she painted them. She still had rabbits and things then. And I went as Pigling Bland in my gasmask, and made cardboard ears. And she gave me a first edition of Pigling Bland and autographed it. So that is one of my most treasured possessions.

Jennifer Forsythe (born 1931)

> *A Lake District year offered children plenty of opportunity to join in traditional festivities such as Rushbearing in Grasmere and Ambleside, Rose Queen celebrations, maypole dancing, fancy dress parades, tableaux, pace-egging and sports days. Empire Day was also celebrated.*
> *Rushbearing, dating back over 500 years, celebrated the strewing of fresh rushes on the earthen floors of churches. Although once commonly celebrated, only a handful of places including Ambleside, Grasmere, Great Musgrave, Urswick and Warcop in Cumbria continue the old tradition. Children carry the 'bearings' through the streets. Ambleside's bearings include the Harp of David, the Globe and the Churchwardens' staves.*

They were decorated with flowers from the garden

We were taught the Rushbearing hymn as soon as we could learn to read and write and sing. We had our own bearings in those days although there were bigger bearings kept at the joiners. They used to keep them over the year and repair them if they needed repairing and bring them out for the Rushbearing. They needed mossing and the bigger boys and older people used to go down to the churchyard and gather moss. The smaller children used to have their own little bearings and decorate them at home. They were decorated with flowers from the garden or wild flowers.

John Ellis (born 1910)

We had gingerbread

For Rushbearing everyone had a new dress and new shoes. Saturday was the Rushbearing procession – through the town and then to church. We had gingerbread, and the town band played and kept on playing for dancing in the park. After school on the Monday was a tea party and sports.

Joan Newby (born 1922)

> *In Grasmere, rushes are laid on a linen sheet carried by six Rushbearing Maidens wearing a green smock over a white blouse and on their heads either a hat or a circlet of flowers. The bearings are mostly wound with rushes and flowers are added as decoration. Bearings such as 'Peace', which was first carried in 1919, are very large. Other subjects include St Oswald's crown and hand, the Creed, Hope and the Maypole.*

Girl Guides' camp at Dove Nest above Windermere, early 1920s.

Maypole dancing in
Ambleside, 1920s.

I've never missed a Grasmere Rushbearing

I've never missed a Grasmere Rushbearing ... I have been in eighty-four. We used to do our
Rushbearings with moss, they do them now with rushes. We used to do them all with moss
and then stick flowers in, and we used to stick rushes in as well. But I used to carry one of
Mrs Rawnsley's; she had some special ones and I always carried Moses in the Bullrushes and it
was a little doll in a little cot thing made of water lily leaves and it had water lilies on it and it
had a china doll in it.

Marjorie Dodgson (born 1914)

We picked our own wild flowers to put on them

My father used to cut the rushes. He had a boat on the lake, used to go down and cut the
rushes and bring them all up here and we did them in what we called the music room at the
back of the house. We picked our own wild flowers to put on them. Of course, in those years
you could put wild flowers, in fact they got extremely annoyed if you put anything else except
wild flowers on it.

Shelagh Griffin (born 1920)

Ambleside
Rushbearing
procession led by
Miss Routledge,
1920s.

Grasmere
Rushbearing
maidens.

Ambleside pupils
performing drill
in the open air
to celebrate the
coronation of King
George V, 1911.

Eyes right and salute the flag

I don't suppose children know what Empire Day is now. We had a flagpole in the yard, and on Empire Day we all had to form up in proper lines and march past and eyes right and salute the flag. You see that was a tradition that was always kept up. We gave a proper military type of salute.

Percy Middleton (born 1904)

> *From the 1970s, Grizedale Forest became world famous because of the Forestry Commission's imaginative policy of combining forestry with recreation. There are now more than seventy sculptures scattered through the forest created with whatever materials were at hand: slate, stone, spruce or oak, either carved or sawn into blocks, balks and battens. Grizedale's centrepiece, sadly now closed, was the Theatre in the Forest.*

We were able to invite the finest pianists in the world

We did not want this theatre to become a theatre for one section of the community. We wanted to make it a theatre which would cut right across the wide spectrum of audience potential, and we've always promoted a wide range of events – we do classical music, ballet, jazz, natural history, folk music, drama and mountaineering. Mountaineering's marvellous – put on a mountaineering show in the winter, and these mountaineers, they'll come through five feet of snow to get here!

Once we started going on classical music it became fairly obvious that we had to have a good piano. So we amassed by means of coffee evenings, raffles and what have you the sum of £800, which in those days was quite a lot of money. So I was despatched to London to buy a second-hand piano. I saw Mr Alan who was the boss of Steinways; I told him the situation. I said I've only got £800 and I told them the story about how the theatre started and what we intended to do … and he said, 'Mr Grant – give me your £800; a piano will be delivered on stage in less than a fortnight, pay us the rest (£1,800) when you can, and no interest on the loan.' We paid it off in fourteen months. Since we had that piano we were able to invite the finest pianists in the world – Shura Cherkassky and John Ogden and John Lill, Tamas Vasary, Cécile Oussett.

Bill Grant (born 1919)

> *Lake District entertainment grows from strength to strength with theatres in Keswick and Bowness, as well as excellent amateur drama in towns and villages. The Lake District Summer Music Festival comes round each August and a wealth of local cinemas show all the latest releases. Country shows are as popular as ever, with more modern attractions such as Windermere Air Show, Kendal Calling music festival, and a series of staged outdoor events featuring acrobatics, trapeze and street theatre, all combining to make entertainment a strong feature of Lake District life.*

nine

THE SECOND WORLD WAR

Although the Lake District escaped bombing and destruction during the Second World War, the war still had an enormous impact on local life, sometimes in surprising ways. Those joining the armed forces were sent elsewhere in the United Kingdom as well as overseas, and many of those left behind were redeployed to contribute to the war effort. The Lake District also became a safe haven for hundreds of young evacuees, as well as entire schools and orphanages and even the Royal College of Art.

The Phoney War.

You used to go and see them off on the train

It was a funny time when I think about it. I remember sitting listening to war being declared on the radio and being absolutely petrified and then, sort of nothing happened except an invasion of evacuees and they came and went. But all the lads went ... so that was a big difference for us really. I often think about Windermere Station and what a sad place that was because you used to go and see them off on the train and never really know if they were coming back or not.

Joan Newby (born 1922)

Only those too old, not fit enough to serve or excused from doing so by being in reserved occupations remained at home. Single women were also called up, though they had the choice of doing war work or serving in the forces, and it was the married women, mothers and grandmothers who organised voluntary war work and headed growing families in the absence of their men.

I felt it was prying

When the war started we decided to start a War Comforts Fund, and I had the depot at my house, and we used to send comforts until coupons came in, and then we sent them postal

Joan Newby with her old photographs, some of which are featured in this book.

orders. I was the secretary for that. And I was the representative for the Soldiers, Sailors and Airmen Families Association, [SSAFA] and I also started the WVS [Women's Voluntary Service] in Ambleside, and we had quite a lot of self-evacuated people and I got them roped in. The council always used to ask me if they had an appeal sent to them, like Aid to Russia, Aid to China and the Spitfire Fund, and St Dunstan's and Salvation Army Huts for Troops, and I organised all these appeals. As a volunteer member of SSAFA I used to have some horrible cases where servicemen in France thought their wives were going off the rails with the prisoners at Grizedale Camp and I had to send a report. But I didn't like that, I felt it was prying.

Margaret Robinson (born 1893)

Even the most privileged had to face the realities of war. One day a lady in a chauffeur-driven car arrived at the home of the local WVS organiser.

They've taken all my staff, what can I do?

The lady was asked to come in. She said, 'I understand you are the head of the Women's Voluntary Service, well, I want some staff, I want somebody to come and work for me.' 'But,' I said, 'the WVS is not for that.' But she said, 'They've taken all my staff, what can I do?' I said, 'You can shut off a good many of your rooms and cut down and live in a smaller space. That's all you can do.' 'But,' she said, 'I've always been used to staff.' And I said, 'Yes, a lot of people have been used to staff but they haven't got them now.' And I said quite definitely, the Women's Voluntary Service is not for that. So you can imagine the attitude!

Margaret Robinson (born 1893)

> *In 1941 when the Short Brothers aircraft factories on the River Medway in Kent were in increasing danger of attack, the company dispersed its activities to Swindon and Troutbeck Bridge — the latter being solely for the manufacture of the Sunderland Flying Boats.*

Beautiful duck egg blue

The main building was a big hangar, 84,000 square foot, single span, and when it was completed and the last jacks were removed from the span roof, it dropped five eighths of an inch so it was very good. It said something for Harland and Wolff who constructed it. I'm led to believe that it was built under a lot of the usual opposition from the Friends of the Lake District with specific instructions that when it had fulfilled its purpose it had to be pulled down.

It's strange how they built flying boats. They started building round about twelve or fourteen of them. I would describe it as a skeleton only, and they were built on what one could only describe it as a boat trailer, ten in the main factory and four in the fabrication shop, and they'd actually drag these things down when we came to put the plane together, for want of a better word. When it got all its skin on, they would drag it off with the tractor, and they would take it to where they were going to put the main plane on. The tail section was always built separate. It was built in parts – the main hull, tail section, then you'd the fin, the two tail wings, as one might say, and the main spars. They used to lift these things on and fit them quite happily like a jigsaw puzzle. From a fourteen-year-old boy's point of view, oh God, it was out of this world, especially when you got interested. Then they'd come along and spray it, finish it, beautiful duck egg blue.

William Harrison (born 1928)

They let us all out of the hangar to watch it go off

They let us all out of the hangar to watch it go off. Then the test pilot gave a demonstration – he came over the village and they tell me that he flew up the main street, more or less hull-down between the trees, right up the main street. They said it was marvellous. It certainly was a great thrill to watch it go off.

Tom Woodward (born 1924)

> *Although Shorts brought much of their workforce with them, the factory provided an opportunity for local men and women to undertake approved war work without having to leave the area.*

There was no roof

It's a wonder we didn't all catch something that we didn't want really because we were in a prefabricated room, it was only just kind of walled off from the factory. There was no roof, and we were by the loading doors where we got all the draughts every time a wagon came to be unloaded. Then they decided that they would put a ceiling on this place, then we couldn't breathe. Then we were near the cutting shop where they cut bakelite and metals and the smell was terrible and the rat-tat-tat of the riveters all day long, that's the atmosphere we were working in.

Joan Fothergill (born 1920)

Lake District farming had to adapt to wartime food production. Ministry inspectors decreed that even upland farmland should be ploughed for growing corn.

It won't ripen

I was ploughing this field and there was snow around the headlands. I said, 'What am I to do with these headlands?' He said, 'Oh, keep ploughing.' It'll come up but it won't ripen. Ploughing was a waste of everybody's time really but we just had it to do because somebody in the office had written that all farmers had to plough so much.

Joe Kegg (born 1912)

You were really supposed to grow it for bread

The first year we just grew corn – and we got to t'back end and it was still green so we had to cut it and eat it for cattle; well, it got to that late you couldn't make it in t'owt, it wouldn't dry nor nothing we got that late. So next two years what we did, we sowed corn or oats or whatever you like and put some clover in it, then mowed it like at hay time. Made grand fodder, you know, but you were really supposed to grow it for bread or summat!

Harry Wilson (born 1908)

Research scientists at the Freshwater Biological Association at Wray Castle were also geared up to wartime food provision. Windermere perch went for tinned perchines, and eel traps provided food for eating as well as material for scientific research.

Sit up all night in a woodchopper's hut

In 1943/44, we had a project going to catch the silver eels coming down the rivers on their way to the Sargasso Sea. Several of us had the job of looking after eel traps on the various rivers, because we were doing an experiment to see if eels could be deflected into traps by barriers of light. I was looking after the trap on the River Crake, so whenever we had more than one and a half inches of rain I had to don all my souwesters and mackintosh gear and cycle from Wray Castle to Nibthwaite at the bottom of Coniston, and sit up all night in a woodchopper's hut switching lights off and on, on this weir, and collecting the eels. I had to empty the eel trap, catch the eels, count them, weigh them, all in the dark with just the light of one little half-blacked out hand torch. Actually I wrote up my thesis for my research during the night in the woodchopper's hut. The eels were sent by lorry to Greenodd probably, and then by train to London.

Joan David (born 1920)

> *Women in the Land Army were not only employed on farms but also by the Forestry Commission's Wartime Timber Supply.*

We had thousands and thousands of pickets

Land Army girls used to do the measuring and the peeling. It was nearly all big [pit] props for the drifts [mines]. And we had thousands and thousands of pickets, we called them, all they were was like a fencing post, and they were taken to the sands to stop the aeroplanes landing in case of an invasion, to stop them landing in Southport and places like that.

Len Crossley (born 1915)

> *For women, war work brought higher wages.*

I thought I was a millionaire!

When I went up to the Land Army I got thirty shillings a week and I thought I was a millionaire!

Mary Hallatsch (born 1912)

> *The Lake District, like the rest of the country, was not exempt from the black-out. Travelling along roads with no lights was hazardous, and trees and lamp-posts were painted with white stripes to make them more visible to cars with their blacked-out headlights.*

No street lighting as such

Car headlights were almost blacked out entirely. The idea was to give the car the minimum little pool of light just in front of its bonnet to enable it to crawl around. To do this a metal insert was made to go inside the front of the headlamp through which the lamp light passed forward and down in front of the vehicle. As there was no street lighting as such permitted, all you had to navigate by was this type of controlled lighting plus any lighting from moonlight.

Stella Ward

> *Rationing affected people in the Lake District as elsewhere. Some people would never dream of breaking the rules, but as it was a farming area there were opportunities to supplement food rations.*

We made sure he got some

We were really self-sufficient in food. During the war people like us, I think, were better off than people in towns because you were your own butcher, you'd your own eggs and things like that. Admittedly, you'd to sacrifice your coupons, your bacon coupons and your butter coupons, but you were better off, I think … the local policeman would come … 'Can I have a pound of butter?' – yes, oh yes, we made sure he got some!

Tom and Hannah Buntin (born 1910 and 1898)

'This is no good; I've got to have more than this'

When my husband came out of the Army in the beginning of 1943 he was absolutely disgusted with the ration. I weighed out his sugar and his butter etc. and I said, 'Now look, that's yours for a week. You've also got your margarine, but my margarine is going to bake something.' 'Oh,' he said, 'This is no good; I've got to have more than this.' 'Well,' I said, 'I haven't any more than this up to now, I've managed with the two of us (that's my daughter), we've managed our ration, and I've never asked for anything over and above, and I'm not going to now. So you'll just have to make the best of it!'

Margaret Robinson (born 1893)

These trees at Ambleside had their trunks painted with white bands to make them more visible in the dark.

> *The number of pigs slaughtered was strictly licensed, to control black-market pork.*

Most people wouldn't dream of looking in a coffin

You had to fill in forms and say how many pigs you had and they were inspected. And the day in Grasmere that the Inspector came round, he started with the pigs at the top of Easedale Farm up there, and unfortunately that farmer had killed a pig, so he was one short, so he was due to be fined. But he managed to get his pigs down to other farmers and when the Inspector went round to other pig keepers, they all had the right number. And if you were in Grasmere that particular day, there were these pigs being driven round from one place to another to make the numbers up! And you could usually get a little bacon if you knew anybody and they knew you wouldn't report them. It was the custom to keep your coffin under the bed and most people wouldn't dream of looking in a coffin … and this was where they kept the sides of bacon!

Meg Walker (born 1921)

> *Lake District hotels were able to access food from various sources, especially if they were in the remoter valleys.*

Eskdale is far out

When we came over to Langdale [to the Old Dungeon Ghyll Hotel] we discovered it was much more difficult catering than it had been in Eskdale [at the Burnmoor Inn], because Eskdale is far out. I don't know whether we ought to say all this! We had a butcher in Seascale and you got more than your rations in Eskdale. More milk as well … but the thing that was really rationed when we started in Eskdale was spirits … a tight ration of spirits. A bottle of whisky, a bottle of gin a month.

Jammie Cross (born 1912)

> *Large numbers of evacuees from the north-east, particularly Newcastle and South Shields, were billeted in Lake District houses and some stayed on after the war was over.*

Mother landed home with sixteen for that night

I remember the evacuees coming into the bus station going on eleven o'clock at night and all these young children from five or six up to fourteen years, there must have been thirty to forty of them, with gasmasks over their shoulders – they looked so lost. I remember them marching down to the Methodist school room and there they were distributed out … it was late at night and mother landed home with sixteen for that night. She put double mattresses on the landings. Next day they were taken back to the Methodist Hall and dished out. We kept two.

Then we had two others, they were little tramps, terrible, they just had what they stood up in and they were filthy dirty and from a family of fourteen … When they came back after Christmas they were dressed in absolute rags and covered from head to foot with sores and scabies. My mother had kitted them out in good clothes. All our toys had to be burned ... and they sealed up the doors and windows and burnt sulphur to fumigate the house. One of my sisters caught scabies as she used to bath them and my mother caught terrible head lice.

Anon. (born 1934)

After the bombing of Barrow-in-Furness in 1941, children were evacuated to the southern Lake District.

We weren't very happy

An auntie was with us because there were two brothers and two sisters going off together. The only reason that my mother would let us go was because she thought that we were all going to be sent to the same place. But when we got to the station all the boys were segregated and the girls had to go with one teacher and I think the boys had to go with the headmaster. We went to Arnside. I can remember us being taken round houses, and I think my sister and I were the last two that were left. I don't know what it was about the two of us – I think perhaps because we were five and seven, they thought we would be more responsibility. And we ended up at a café opposite the station at Arnside with quite an old couple who obviously did not want us. We were there about six or seven months, we weren't very happy.

Tonie Cornforth (born 1934)

Every town and village had its Home Guard made up of men not serving in the forces.

We would have been smashed to smithereens

We had nothing; if there'd been armoured wagons or owt, we would have been smashed to smithereens. I don't know what would have happened if there had been owt, Army would have come and backed you up. But it was Home Guard, a rifle, or a Browning Automatic, or a few grenades, something like that.

Harry Wilson (born 1908)

We were the only platoon like it in the country

There were two platoons in Bowness and Windermere – one based in Windermere and we were based in Bowness ... we had a headquarters down among the boatsheds. We were unique. We were always told we were the only platoon like it in the country. We were completely to do with Lake Windermere, and our job was to patrol the lake and make sure there was no invasion threat from the lake, and also to keep an eye open for lights. Before the war we had had C-Class flying boats landing on the lake, so the Germans knew it was quite feasible to land flying boats, so our little set-up was to prevent this happening. At that time all the heavy industry was down in Lancashire, and this was an easy way of getting to that area if they decided to do it.

Schoolchildren, including evacuees from Tyneside, approaching Underbarrow Primary School. (Cumbria County Council, Kendal Library)

We were about thirty strong. We had four speedboats and two houseboats, all had heavy machine-guns mounted on them, and we used to patrol the lake during the night.

Tom Woodward (born 1924)

The expensive part was the gas

We had one alarm, one scare, in June, when somebody had seen parachutists landing up Far Easedale and the Home Guard were turned out to try and apprehend these. We thought they would be parachutists, and the local church bell was rung which was the warning for everybody that danger was about, and my mother had to cycle to all the outlying farms to warn them that they thought parachutists were landing. But the Home Guard, who were, after all, most of them middle aged or even retired gentlemen, had to rush up Far Easedale in hot, June weather — and when they got there, it was a barrage balloon that had got loose from Barrow and they didn't know quite what to do with it, so they thought the best thing to do was to let all the gas out and fold up the outer covering and take it back with them — only to get very badly hauled over the coals from headquarters because the expensive part was the gas which they had let out!

Meg Walker (born 1921)

> *Grizedale Hall was used as a Prisoner of War camp for captured U-Boat officers. Local people were involved with the camp as guards and in supervising those prisoners who were allowed into the community to work.*

The water-borne Home Guard unit landing with rifles from a gunboat. (Courtesy of Armitt Museum and Library, Ambleside)

Next morning there was an officer missing

On one occasion a U-Boat commander didn't want to be with the other prisoners because he had handed his U-Boat over instead of scuttling it, and he had to be locked away. I was on duty that day in the Hall so we locked him up in the cellar, down in the cells. Well, the rest of the prisoners were running about talking to one another and you knew there was trouble. That night we locked them all in and next morning there was an officer missing. The second-in-command was missing. He'd got out through the wire and they put a search party out. The Home Guard caught him, but he started running, so one of the Home Guards shot him. He was put on a stretcher and they brought him down to camp and when he got down to the camp he died. He was only a young fellow of about thirty-two with two children and he was buried in Hawkshead churchyard. After the war his mother took him back to Germany.

Ernest Ridgeway, prison guard at Grizedale Hall (born 1914)

> *For those away from home, the Lake District remained in the memory.*

As far as I was concerned Grasmere was my home town

I served in North Africa with the First Army, then across into Italy attached to the American 5th Army on the Salerno landings. As far as I was concerned, when I was in the army Grasmere was my home town and I drove all over the place in North Africa and Italy on a motorbike and in a jeep and they used to have 'Grasmere' emblazoned on the front of them.

David Scott (born 1923)

Above: Past May Queens celebrating 'Justice and Freedom', May 1945.

Left: Fundraising for 'Returned Forces Week', 1945.

VE-Day was celebrated as energetically in the Lake District as elsewhere.

A fancy dress parade

At the end of the war we had this big 'Returned Forces Week' making money for the lads coming back and they had a whole week of events … and we had a programme of events for VE-Day, whist drives, concerts, dances and a fancy dress parade in the village – and they all hired costumes. Harry Stubbs had on a nightie and a nightcap and sat in an old bath chair, and Billy Hall dressed up as a nurse and pushed him round, and an old barrel organ was hired and the man went up and down the cinema queues playing to raise money.

Joan Newby (born 1922)

ten

OFFCOMERS

Through the years the Lake District has absorbed new populations. With improvements in transport even more people came to find work or seek refuge and many have simply chosen to live in the Lake District. Such people are known locally as 'offcomers', and have gradually outnumbered those born and bred in the area. Being an offcomer is not always easy, but most have been welcomed by 'locals' whose neighbours they have become.

Big engineering works have often required a labour force that could not be satisfied locally. The construction and maintenance of the Thirlmere aqueduct between the Lake District and Manchester was just such an enterprise a century ago, and the workers and their families became absorbed into the local communities.

They soon grew into little country children

When I came [to teach at Ambleside] there had just been an influx into the village of workmen and their families who were working on the Thirlmere aqueduct … which altered the complexion of the village entirely. They came from towns in Lancashire and Yorkshire, but they soon grew into little country children and enjoyed the sports and the different kind of life they lived and got on with the other children quite well.

Alice Blezzard (born 1880)

I'll get him married before I finish with him!

We had two of the men that worked in the [Thirlmere] tunnel. They were really Gloucestershire miners, and they took me one night up to the tunnel … the fellow picked me up and carried me, that was a few days before the tunnel went through and it was wonderful. The two ends met, just like that! Those men lived with us for about two years. One of them couldn't write and he had a sweetheart – and my auntie was a devil and she used to write his love letters for him. She said, 'I'll get him married before I am finished with him!'

Edith Benson (born 1877)

A section of the Thirlmere pipeline being taken up Chapel Hill, Ambleside.

At the end of the First World War, the jobs that women had taken reverted to the men folk, and at that time some women came to the Lakes in search of work.

The most beautiful place I'd ever seen

When I came to Ambleside I thought it was the most beautiful place I'd ever seen and the people all seemed to be rich … everybody seemed well off. There was people out of work I suppose, and some people were just ordinary, but I couldn't see that; there wasn't the real poverty here that there was in Wigton, my home town.

Mabel Middleton (born 1910)

At the end of the Second World War enemy soldiers who had been prisoners of war in camps in the Lake District sometimes got jobs locally and opted to remain in the area.

I never regret it

I was transferred to Bela Camp in Milnthorpe. Camp 104 they called it. After the armistice I started to work. I and five mates of mine, we went to Goodacres carpet factory in Holme Mills. We used to bike in on a morning. For the first fortnight we had a guard with us, and after that we didn't ... We didn't know what we should expect – because although it was after the war, you know it was not so easy for a German prisoner of war, but they were very, very nice those people, and I can't say anything against them. I had been treated very well and still have friends there. Then the repatriation started but I decided then to stay in this country for a while, work on a farm which I had been used to. I took the choice to be discharged from the army and took a job in early December 1945. And I liked it very much. I used to work forty-eight cows and full milk units, and that's where I met my wife, Mary Bowe. On October 6th 1950 we got married, and I came to Ashton Cottage, where I've been ever since ... and I never regret it. I have been here very well received, and so I can't speak highly enough of the British people.

Heinz Hallatsch (born 1924)

The wars of the twentieth century brought all sorts of people to the Lake District. Refugees found sanctuary in the area in both the First and Second World Wars and at the start of the Second World War, large numbers of children were evacuated to the Lake District from Newcastle, Sunderland and London, and more locally from Barrow-in-Furness. Their new lives were very different.

We had some Belgian refugees

During the [First World] war we had some Belgian refugees living down here at Low Nook [Ambleside] and my father employed some of those people to work in the bobbin mill during the First World War, because some of our men had gone, had left for the war.

Bernard Horrax (born 1896)

'Haven't you got any boys?'

I came to Ambleside in the beginning of July 1940 as an evacuee with Dame Allan's Girls' School from Newcastle-on-Tyne. I suppose there must have been about 200 of us – all girls, with teachers, one or two parents and helpers. There was also Dame Allan's Boys' School who evacuated to Windermere. We arrived at the station in Windermere. We didn't know what route we had taken because all the signs had been taken down from the railway stations ... we walked down to the St Mary's vicarage gardens. It was a lovely day, and we were given tea I think on the lawn, and we were also each given a carrier bag which contained iron rations. I can remember some hard biscuits, and a tin of condensed milk and a tin of corned beef that we called bully beef. Then we were taken by bus to Ambleside, and to the hall at the back of the Queen's Hotel where there were WVS-type ladies. The names were called out, and some of us had asked to be with friends, so my name was called out, and my friend Joan, and this lady took us outside and we got into quite an old car, I think it was an Austin 7, and took us down to Waterhead, and we went to Over Borrans which belonged to the MacIver family ... there was a big house at the top of the drive and Mrs MacIver came to the door. We were two girls, both thirteen, standing there in our school uniform, and Mrs MacIver looked at us and looked at the lady helper, and said, 'Haven't you got any boys?' So the lady helper said, 'Well I'm sorry, but it's a girl's school.' 'Oh well,' she said, 'never mind.' So we were taken in and actually put in the care of the cook. There was also a maid, a gardener and a chauffeur and handyman. It was holiday time, but we did go up to the Kelsick Grammar School most mornings and various things were arranged for us, a few outings, and then when school started the local pupils from Kelsick Grammar School went in the morning, from about half past eight until one o'clock, and we went at one o'clock and stayed until about half past five.

Maureen Watson (born 1926)

> *Many refugees were assisted by the Quakers, including the Freiberger family from Vienna, who had fled Hitler only to be bombed out of their new home in London and again in Coventry.*

They were wonderful to us

After the November air raid on Coventry we tried to get away. A Quaker social worker wrote to Quakers in Windermere, a Mr and Mrs Stanley Davies. He was a sculptor of woodwork and made beautiful furniture. They were wonderful to us. They treated my children as if they were their grandparents. He tried to find us a job. He suggested Langdale Estate and my husband was hired and looked after the electricity and the water. That is how we came to live in Langdale.

Ilse Freiberger, a Jewish Austrian refugee (born 1909)

> *Mr Freiberger put his skills as an engineer to excellent use in wartime Langdale, harnessing water power to bring the valley its first electricity supply which powered the workshop where he mended cars and farm machinery, often in exchange for a rabbit or some eggs or butter. This in turn helped his wife Ilse to stretch meagre food rations further for guests at the Gateway Hotel, where her Viennese-style cakes and pastries were soon legendary. Their son, Fred, went to Langdale School.*

Being Jewish this was an interesting experience

The whole school at Langdale would march up to the village church on special days like Ash Wednesday or Good Friday … and there would be a lot of pomp and ceremony in the Christmas period. Being Jewish, this was an interesting experience. I played virtually every role in nativity plays, starting out as a child giving his most beloved toy to the Christ child. I remember walking the whole length of the main aisle of the church, carrying my 'Jumbo' – my arms were stretched forward and tears running down my eyes because I didn't know that this was just a play and that I was going to get Jumbo back. And then in subsequent years, I played the shepherds and I played a wise man and so on. And it was a very liberal education, very understanding. The vicar made sure that he made reference to the Old Testament as well, so that we were very comfortable … we all went to school together, so it was very ecumenical.

Fred Freiberger (born 1938)

Above: Evacuated pupils collecting waste paper at Millans Park, Ambleside.

Right: Edward and Ilse Freiberger with their children, Fred and Ann, in Langdale in the late 1940s.

Adult German Jews who were already living in England when war broke out in 1939 were classed as enemy aliens, and for a time many were interned in camps in the Isle of Man. However, after they were released, although they could visit the Lake District, some restrictions on movement continued to be applied.

We had to part at Clappersgate

To travel, you had to get permission to leave London. And of course when I arrived in Ambleside I had to report to the police in Ambleside that I am here … I think [they] would phone ahead. My girlfriend had a research job at the Freshwater Biological Association at Wray Castle, which at that time was in Lancashire and it was out of bounds as far as I was concerned because of Grizedale Prisoner of War Camp. So when I managed to get a trip up north to see my girlfriend I wasn't allowed to enter Lancashire. I had to stay the other side of the county boundary in Clappersgate. So I had to arrange that she would cycle from Wray to Clappersgate and we could spend the day in Westmorland so we had the whole of Langdale and Ambleside at our disposal. But then in the evening, when we'd had the day, we had to part at Clappersgate! That was in 1941 and '42, but by 1943 things had changed and I was allowed to actually visit her at Wray Castle.

Vernon David (born 1920)

Stanley and Emily Davies at their home in Windermere, where they helped resettle Jewish refugees.

The Second World War also brought workers to the Lake District involved in manufacturing equipment for the forces. Short Brothers brought the workforce from their bombed-out factory at Rochester.

We didn't have a very good reception

We didn't have a very good reception from the Windermere people. There was a reason for that. As you know, during the war the government could commandeer places and accommodation for whoever they moved about the country, and the billeting officer had been around the dwellings in Windermere sometime before, finding out what accommodation they had. We arrived in Windermere and were taken to our various billets and the people that we were billeted with were very angry because the officer had just been round that afternoon telling them that whoever they had in the accommodation had to get out, right away, because these people were to be put in there. And in some instances some of our people had to get a policeman to make the people take the people in.

Ivor Greening (born 1910)

The Windermere Boys at a film show in the Entertainment Hall at Calgarth Estate, 1945. (Courtesy of Another Space and 45 Aid Society (Holocaust Survivors UK))

The pre-fab housing supplied for workers at the Short Brothers factory at Troutbeck Bridge played an important post-war role in 1945 as temporary home for several hundred Jewish boys (the Windermere Boys) who had survived the Nazi labour and concentration camps. For many of these boys their time at Windermere is fondly remembered for the welcome they received from the local people as well as the peaceful environment which helped them to begin the process of reintegration into society. One Polish Jewish survivor of labour camps and Auschwitz recalled arriving at Windermere after a flight from Prague.

The joy we experienced was something almost indescribable

We came to Windermere on the 14th of August 1945, and the joy we experienced was something almost indescribable. A summer's day in Windermere. We'd not seen such happiness, such wonderful scenery, such wonderful countryside – all we'd seen was the most miserable existence in the world, bereft of anything of greenery or of anything else. And here we could enjoy. And the first thing they did – and I think this was a very wise policy – they brought us back to the atmosphere that we had at home which was the teaching of faith, of our faith, without bitterness. Not going into the past too much, but recalling the wonderful days, going back to this atmosphere of the learning of the Jewish home, of the faith and so forth. And I think this brought us back memories, the happy memories, in order to crowd out and push away the painful past as much as possible.

We were kept together, but not as a large group, because eventually in November we were taken away from Windermere to different places, like Liverpool, Manchester, Gateshead,

London, and I think one or two other places as well. And I, for some reason, decided to go to Manchester. I just liked the crowd that was going to Manchester.

Mayer Hersch (born 1926)

> *The Lake Distict has continued to welcome refugees during the post-war years. In 1979 Ambleside hosted a number of Vietnamese boat people. These refugees were supported by the Ockenden Venture.*

They were a bit intimidated by the mountains

The village took this project for the boat people to its heart. There are a lot of very good hearted people in Ambleside and we'd all been reading in the papers about the plight of the boat people, and there was a lot of hand wringing going on but one didn't feel one was able to do anything. And then you heard that there was a house round the corner being opened up, but it needed everything – beds, bedding and all sorts of equipment ... In the first place, one family came, a man and his wife and five young children. I was paid to teach English to the Vietnamese. I had no experience of teaching English as a foreign language but I was a teacher, an infant teacher, so I did what I could. The children of course were gorgeous and quite unlike anybody else we'd got living in the village, and the older ones went to school.

Families came and went, nobody stayed for longer than six months. They weren't thrilled to come to the Lake District, a lot of them were city people and they didn't like the countryside; they were a bit intimidated by the mountains. They didn't like the weather. They found it very grey, very cold. They had no concept of hanging your washing out and then getting it in when it was raining. They would only hang their washing out if it was an uninterrupted blue sky with lots of sunshine.

Judith Shingler (born 1949)

Teacher Judith Shingler and her son Stuart, with two of her Vietnamese refugee pupils.

For a long time opportunities to work and play in the outdoors have drawn people from the industrial towns of the north. The creation of the Lake District National Park in 1951 increased the recreational appeal of the Lake District, as did the famous fell-walking guidebooks' author Alfred Wainwright, who first visited the Lake District while working in Blackburn, and later came to live and work in Kendal as Borough Treasurer. The pressure caused by increasing number of walkers generated the need for landscape maintenance and management which provided employment opportunities for offcomers such as John Wyatt, the National Park's first warden and later first Chief Ranger, who had come to live in the area as a trainee forester.

I was the only interviewee without a beard!

I was born near Manchester. I got my first job as a copyboy in the Manchester office of the *Daily Telegraph*. At the age of sixteen, I saw a job advertised in the Lake District as a trainee forester and I got it. After the war I came back to the Lake District and had a number of jobs before I saw the advertisement for the first National Park warden in 1960. It was a new post and it sounded exciting. There were several hundred applicants, but I thought that I had an advantage as I was living here and I knew the area. After I got the job, Lady Lowther, who was on the interview committee, told me that she had voted for me because I was the only interviewee without a beard!

John Wyatt (born 1925)

Improved public transport brought growing numbers of weekend walkers, who then dreamed of coming to live permanently.

I'd always had a great love for this part of the world

We came to live here in October 1966. Like a lot of other people it had always been my ambition to retire permanently to the Lake District if that were possible, because I'd always had a great love for this part of the world having visited it first in 1928 … we came a tremendous lot in the '30s to Langdale and Borrowdale, Seatoller … we were very fond of walking, we were in the Rover Scouts, which might explain a lot.

Syd Prentice, artist (born 1911)

For regular visitors, the magic never fades.

It's like coming home

The great joy of the Lakes to me is that it's all within a thirty-mile diameter circle, so you go up one place and you see another mountain just across there – 'well that's where I was' or 'where I want to go next week'. There's nowhere else in the world quite like it, I've been to the Alps and walked in the hills there, but you can't climb from the bottom to the top in a day, you have to go up in a lift and start from somewhere higher up. The Lake District is very magical in that respect. I just get a thrill as I drive over the brow of the hill above Windermere station and see the lake before me – it's like coming home.

David Buck (born 1934)

> *Some visitors still come in search of a country retreat and have bought cottages as second homes or holiday lets, with the consequence that house prices have risen so high they are unaffordable for local people. In some areas well over half the houses have become second homes, and many village communities are no longer viable, with local services disappearing.*

The young people have gone away

There isn't the close feeling of community that there used to be in the old days, and we're not such a balanced community. There aren't nearly as many young working people in proportion as there used to be – there are far more elderlies, because a lot of the younger people have had to go away for work because they couldn't get housing here. That's been one of our difficulties. As houses come up for sale they become very, very expensive and they're bought by offcomers as holiday houses and the young people have gone away. There are not nearly as many children as there were. I think it's a pity because we haven't got the community activities that there were in the old days … one misses that close affinity where you knew everybody.

Agnes Inman (born 1915)

> *By contrast, the arrival of new blood or retired offcomers has brought in vital skills and new enthusiasms.*

We weren't accepted very easily

1934 was the year we came to Ambleside. I was twenty-six I think, and newly married, and a Londoner! Very much so. I found it a bit different up here and we were rather offcomers you know. We weren't accepted very easily, but the village needed another doctor.

Mary Mylechreest (born 1907)

It was always my intention to live in the Lake District

I came from Preston in Lancashire … but my parents had always come to the Lake District – they'd had a boat on the lake before the war, and then we had a caravan on White Cross Bay and came every weekend. It was always my intention to live in the Lake District. So when we got married, my husband and I decided we would look for a business in the Lake District … and we bought a restaurant in Ambleside … and we've been here ever since.

Judith Shingler (born 1949)

A lot of them were not what you might call locals

The Lake District Horticultural Society members were just people interested in gardening. You see, a lot of them were not what you might call real locals. They were people who'd retired to this area after doing other things; found themselves with a garden, interested in it, and interested in learning more and developing it.

Marjorie Bowker (born 1909)

In recent years, many Eastern Europeans have come to work locally and a few have made the Lake District their home.

I feel like I'm now doing something for this community

I like it here. It was quite easy to get a job. I feel like part of this community now, because I'm also a retained firefighter – there's only, I think, twelve retained firefighters in this village. And I feel like I'm now doing something for this community. So that's pretty good.

Waldik Gajdowski (born 1969)

It's everything that a human being wants, that's Ambleside

If you compare a town like Ambleside to a town in Poland, Ambleside is more intellectual, you can do so many things … you can go for a walk, you can travel, there is Windermere train station, Manchester airport, everything. The crime in Ambleside? Actually, there is no crime. It's everything that a human being wants, that's Ambleside. That is true!

Jacek Zych (born 1979)

Other titles published by The History Press

The Guide to the Mysterious Lake District
GEOFF HOLDER

This is the guide to everything strange, mysterious and uncanny that has occurred in the beautiful and rugged Lake District. Every historic site and ancient monument is explored – including stone circles, ancient cairns and crumbling stations – along with the many hidden treasures to be found in the area. From the strange histories of the Romantic poets to modern sightings of ghosts, UFOs and monsters in the lakes, it is an indispensable companion for the traveller about to delve into the mysterious realms of the Lake District.

978 0 7524 4987 6

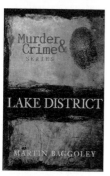

Murder & Crime Lake District
MARTIN BAGGOLEY

Drawing on a wide selection of sources and illustrated with more than fifty images, this collection of grisly tales explores the darker side of the Lake District's past. It features the tale of the 'Keswick Imposter', who seduced and bigamously married a young lady of Buttermere before being hanged at Castile for fraud, a story which was the inspiration for Melvyn Bragg's *The Maid of Buttermere*. With murders, hangings, kidnapping and violence, this book is sure to captivate and horrify everyone interested in the criminal history of the area.

978 0 7524 4805 3

Cumbria Curiosities
ROBERT WOODHOUSE

Cumbria Curiosities brings together a series of unusual, intriguing and extraordinary buildings, structures, incidents and people from all parts of the county. Included in these pages are the Rebel's Tree at Clifton – setting for the last battle on English soil; Maryport's church, where the pulpit is in the form of a ship's prow; a hilltop tower at Hampsfell which has poetic advice for travellers; and Millom's Gallows Field, where felons were executed in the seventeenth century. This volume tells an alternative history of Cumbria that will fascinate residents and visitors alike.

978 0 7509 5078 7

Voices from Barrow and Furness
ALICE LEACH

This book draws together memories of life on the Furness peninsula from a wide range of people who have fascinating tales to tell. Among their number are shopkeepers, an MP, a vicar, an undertaker, a zookeeper, a councillor, and entrepreneur and a midwife, to name just a few. The stories they recall, collected by members of the Barrow Oral History Group, will rekindle memories for anyone who has lived in this area for more than a few years, and will be an eye-opener for any new arrivals who want to find out more about the history of Furness.

978 0 7509 4743 5

Visit our website and discover thousands of other History Press books.
www.thehistorypress.co.uk

The History Press